Ethnographic Sorcery

Ethnographic Sorcery

HARRY G. WEST

The University of Chicago Press ❋ Chicago and London

The University of Chicago Press, Chicago 60637
The University of Chicago Press, Ltd., London
© 2007 by The University of Chicago
All rights reserved. Published 2007
Printed in the United States of America
16 15 14 13 12 11 10   3 4 5

Library of Congress Cataloging-in-Publication Data
West, Harry G.
  Ethnographic sorcery / Harry G. West.
    p. cm.
  Includes bibliographical references and index.
  ISBN-13: 978-0-226-89397-6 (cloth : alk. paper)
  ISBN-13: 978-0-226-89398-3 (pbk. : alk. paper)
  ISBN-10: 0-226-89397-9 (cloth : alk. paper)
  ISBN-10: 0-226-89398-7 (pbk. : alk. paper)
    1. Makonde (African people)—Rites and ceremo-
nies.   2. Makonde (African people)—Religion.
3. Makonde (African people)—Politics and govern-
ment.   4. Witchcraft—Mozambique—Mueda Dis-
trict.   5. Magic—Mozambique—Mueda District.
6. Culture—Mozambique—Muede District—Semiotic
models.   7. Mueda District (Mozambique)—Social
conditions.   8. Mueda District (Mozambique)—
Politics and government.   I. Title.
  DT3328.M35W46 2007
  305.896′397—dc22
                                    2006030054

♾ The paper used in this publication meets the mini-
mum requirements of the American National Standard
for Information Sciences—Permanence of Paper for
Printed Library Materials, ANSI Z39.48-1992.

For Catherine

Contents

Preface

Having traveled downstream by canoe, a magician comes ashore to discover the charred remains of a fire god's temple in Jorge Luis Borges's short story "The Circular Ruins" (1970). Though he knows nothing of his own past, he is animated by the desire to achieve "the most arduous task a man [can] undertake, . . . to mould the incoherent and vertiginous matter dreams are made of," in short, "to dream a man . . . and insert him into reality." He dreams a beating heart, "perceiv[ing] it, liv[ing] it, from many distances and many angles." Over the course of the following year, bit by bit, he gives form to a complete man, into which the fire god breathes life. Following the god's mandate, the magician—all the while haunted by the sense that what is happening has happened before—instructs his progeny in the rites of the fire cult, vacates his memory of all traces of his years of apprenticeship, and sends him off to inhabit an abandoned temple downstream. With the passage of time, the magician hears word from two boatmen traveling upstream of a man who walks on fire without being burned. He remembers being told by the fire god that all but he and fire itself would see his phantom dream-child as flesh and blood. "Not to be a man, to be the projection of another man's dream, what a feeling of humiliation, of vertigo!" he laments. Soon thereafter, the sky grows rose-colored, and flames converge on the magician and his temple. For an instant, he considers taking refuge in the river, before perceiving that death is coming "to crown his old age and absolve him of his labours." The flames engulf him, caress him; "with relief, with humiliation, with terror, he under[stands] that he too [is] a mere appearance, dreamt by another."

The story I tell in a previously published work, entitled *Kupilikula: Governance and the Invisible Realm in Mozambique* (2005a), is similar to Borges's. On the Mueda plateau, it is said that sorcerers invisibly feed on the well-being of their rivals, neighbors, and/or kin. By rendering themselves invisible, they transcend the world inhabited by ordinary people, producing and inhabiting an invisible realm from which they gain powerful perspective on the visible—a platform from which to elaborate and bring to fruition ghastly visions of carnage that feed their insatiable appetites. These acts, however, do not go unchallenged. Responsible figures of authority, including healers, lineage councilors, settlement heads, and even contemporary village presidents, are also said to be capable of entering into the invisible realm of sorcery. Acting as "sorcerers of construction," they transcend not only the world inhabited by ordinary Muedans but also that of "sorcerers of ruin," fixing the latter in *their* gaze, monitoring and controlling sorcerers' activities, unmaking sorcerers' acts, and remaking the world in accordance with their own visions of a world reordered.[1] What appears to one a constructive act may appear to another ruinous, and so the game of one-upmanship, comprising transcendent maneuvers that Muedans gloss with the verb *kupilikula* (to invert, to reverse, to overturn, to negate, to annul, to undo), continues in perpetuity.

As I describe in this previous work, *kupilikula* is a game into which everyone is drawn. When Catholic missionaries to the plateau region condemned Muedan sorcery beliefs and practices and offered their own vision of the forces defining earthly and heavenly domains, Muedans heard their words as condemnations of ruinous sorcery but, simultaneously, as the enactment of a novel form of sorcery of construction. Similarly, when the revolutionary socialist leaders of the Mozambican Liberation Front (A Frente de Libertação de Moçambique, or FRELIMO) dismissed Muedan talk of sorcery as a form of "false consciousness" and articulated their scientific socialist agenda for a transformed, postcolonial society, Muedans heard in their words claims to a transcendent vision such as the ones long professed by healers, lineage councilors, and settlement heads. Ironically, in reading missionaries and nationalists *as* (counter)sorcerers, Muedans fixed these figures in *their* own sights, unmaking their claims, and remaking the worlds that together they inhabited.

Notwithstanding the similarity between Borges's story and my ethnography, in this volume I identify, not with the author of "The Circular Ruins," but instead with the magician protagonist, for in making sorcery an object of ethnographic study in that earlier work—in exploring what Michael Jackson might refer to as the "existential uses and consequences" (1996: 6) of Muedan sorcery discourse—I myself (re)made Muedans and their world in accordance with a vision of my own elaboration. In this work, I explore the epistemological paradox arising from the ethnographic study of sorcery. My ethnography—my transcendent maneuver—scarcely ended the game of transcendence, it would seem. I too became the object of scrutiny by those who would unmake, and remake, me—by those who would challenge my vision and reinvent the world in accordance with their own. This volume tells the story of a dawning perception that all that happens has happened before—that the ethnographer, like those he dreams, is himself susceptible to being dreamt.

Acknowledgments

This volume draws upon research conducted with the financial support of the Land Tenure Center (University of Wisconsin–Madison), the Fulbright-Hays Program, the United States Institute of Peace, the Wenner-Gren Foundation, the Economic and Social Research Council (United Kingdom), and the British Academy. This volume was written together with (in fact, in early drafts was a component part of) my first book, *Kupilikula: Governance and the Invisible Realm in Mozambique* (2005a). I therefore owe thanks here to all those I acknowledged in *Kupilikula*. A special thanks, however, goes to the American Council of Learned Societies/Social Science Research Council/ National Endowment for the Humanities and to the Program in Agrarian Studies at Yale University, each of which provided fellowships to release me from teaching responsibilities to focus on writing. Participants in the Program in Agrarian Studies seminar provided a particularly stimulating environment in which to develop my thoughts. Principal among them was Eric Worby, with whom I exchanged ideas on a weekly basis during the most crucial periods of production of the pieces that became this volume. Portions of the book were presented in the Franz Boas Seminar in the Department of Anthropology at Columbia University, the weekly seminar in the Program in Agrarian

Studies at Yale University, and the weekly seminar in the Department of Anthropology at the London School of Economics, each of which afforded stimulating commentary. Partial or whole drafts were read by Barney Bate, Alex Bortolot, Matthew Engelke, Carol Greenhouse, Charles Hirschkind, Paolo Israel, Shelley Khadem, Tracy Luedke, Thomas Dodie McDow, Parvathi Raman, and Karolina Szmagalska, each of whom provided constructive criticism. Valuable feedback was also given by Don Brenneis and Michael Lambek in their capacities as readers for the University of Chicago Press. My thanks also go to everyone at the University of Chicago Press, including David Brent, Elizabeth Branch Dyson, and Pamela Bruton. Once again, I owe my deepest debt of gratitude to the Muedans among whom I worked, and especially to those who collaborated with me in my research, namely, Marcos Agostinho Mandumbwe, Eusébio Tissa Kairo, and Felista Elias Mkaima.

Misunderstanding

He lives by imagination and wit and what he sells are metaphors.
«LANDEG WHITE, *Magomero* (1987: 250), in reference to Jagaja, a self-proclaimed "native doctor" selling remedies in the marketplace »

"Andiliki," he said, "I think you misunderstand." Years later, the words still ring in my ears. That he addressed me by my Shimakonde name[1] reminded everyone in the room just how close to them all I had become and, perhaps, just how much I *did* understand of the history and culture of the residents of the Mueda plateau in northern Mozambique, among whom I had been studying for nearly a year. Still, I had gotten it all wrong, he told me.

I had just finished giving a talk to an audience of some two dozen people assembled in the provincial office of the Cultural Heritage Archives (Arquivos do Patrimônio Cultural, or ARPAC) in Pemba. It was my third presentation in a series of three, given in late 1994 at the request of the archive's provincial director. As I had benefited greatly in my field research from the assistance of an ARPAC staff researcher, namely Eusébio Tissa Kairo, I had been asked to give something back to the institution. Although each and every one of ARPAC's half dozen staff researchers had far more ethnographic fieldwork experience than I, none had much formal training in anthropological theory or methodology. I was asked to read through several of their research reports and to address a few topics that I thought might be of interest to them in their continuing professional work.

The chosen topic for my third talk, a brief introduction to the subfield of symbolic anthropology by way of Victor Turner's essay "Symbols in Ndembu Ritual" (1967), was doubly motivated. While ARPAC researchers filled their reports with detailed ethnographic data, they hesitated, I noticed, to analyze or interpret what their informants told them. I wished to inspire them to move beyond the cataloguing of data and the verbatim quotation of informants that characterized their publications. Turner, I informed them, illustrated this through his analysis of the *nkang'a* (girls' puberty) ritual. Clearly, according to Turner, the sap of the *mudyi* (milk) tree at the ritual's center symbolized the milk of the initiate's ripening breasts; beyond this, Turner's informants told him that the tree symbolized unity—between the initiate and her mother, between the members of the initiate's matrilineage, and between all Ndembu more generally. Because, however, the ritual as Turner saw it actually produced and enacted tensions in each of these relationships—separating daughter from mother and pitting matrilineage against matrilineage and Ndembu women against Ndembu men—he concluded that, despite Ndembu exegesis (or lack thereof), the tree also symbolized the social tensions that the ritual mediated. I wondered what my audience would make of Turner's audacious conclusion that anthropologists such as he—*and* such as they—might see and interpret a ritual event unencumbered by the "interests" and "sentiments" that "impair [the native's] understanding of the total situation" (27).

The second motive for my chosen topic was my desire to present a piece of my own ethnographic work in progress. The ARPAC provincial director had opened my series of talks to a public audience in order to raise awareness in the provincial capital of the institution's work. Notwithstanding this, most in the audience had some degree of familiarity with the communities among whom I had worked—some, even, with my project itself. Many were government functionaries who worked in the provincial departments of education or culture and with whom I had previously consulted. Most had been born and raised on the Mueda plateau and maintained strong ties there. Situated as they were between Mueda and the larger world, they constituted an ideal group, I thought, with whom to undertake a bit of what Steven Feld has called "dialogical editing" (1987) of my emergent ethnography. Consequently, in the second part of my talk, I made use of Turner's ideas to engage with material collected in the course of my own research on the Mueda plateau.

I briefly summarized for my audience what most already knew: when a lion was seen in or around a plateau village, people often speculated that it was not an ordinary lion, not an *ntumi wa ku mwitu* (bush lion); rather, they often suggested, it was an *ntumi wa nkaja* (a settlement lion), meaning either that it was a sorcerer who had turned into a lion, in which case it might also be called an *ntumi munu* (lion-person), or that it was made by a sorcerer, in which case it might also be called an *ntumi wa kumpika* (a fabricated lion). Sorcery lions devoured the flesh of sorcerers' rivals, neighbors, and kin, sometimes through visible attacks and sometimes through invisible ones that produced chronic illness.

To deal with such a lion—most of my audience, again, already knew—a specialist was summoned to discern the lion's true nature and to prepare medicinal substances that rendered the beast vulnerable to hunters. At the same time, people continued to deliberate on the identity of the person associated with the lion and on the identity of the lion's intended victim. Employing Turner's theoretical framework, I suggested to my audience that, as Muedans examined who among them might be envious of whom—who sought to appropriate the wealth of others without honest work; who transgressed egalitarian norms by failing to share as they should; in short, who among them was "predator" and who was "prey"—their anger and distrust were infused with, and heightened by, their fear of the lion. In Turner's terms, the lion, as symbol, connected the ideological and sensory poles of their experience—not only of the hunt for the lion but also of the broader sociohistorical drama (sometimes including the lynching of those subsequently accused of sorcery).

I reminded my audience that there was more to the story than this, however. According to Turner, "the simplest property [of a ritual symbol] is that of condensation," meaning that a symbol may represent "many things and actions" at once (1967: 28). On the plateau, the lion not only symbolized social predation, I postulated, it also symbolized nobility and power. I reminded them that among the most respected and feared Makonde elders, historically, were *vahumu* (sing. *humu*). Beyond their duties as matrilineage councilors in the visible quotidian realm, these elders also monitored the hidden realm of *uwavi* (sorcery), bringing their power to bear on sorcerers whose acts threatened the wellbeing of the settlement. The ritual inductions that *vahumu* were required to undergo had them ingest obscure medicinal substances mixed with, among other things, *lukulungu*—the throat meat of a slain bush lion. While living, *vahumu* "spoke with the voices of lions," who "recognized them as brothers." Upon dying, the corpses of *vahumu* spawned lions that posed a threat to their *makola* (matrilineages) unless their bodies were appropriately treated by fellow *vahumu*.

None of my informants had ever explicitly told me what I was about to say, I now admitted to my audience, but—following Turner's mandate—I suggested that, for residents of the Mueda plateau, the lion not only symbolized both dangerous predator and regal protector but also symbolized a deep ambivalence about the workings of power in the social world. Simultaneously, the lion, as symbol, expressed the ideas that power was necessary to produce and secure the common good and that power constituted an ever-present threat to the community's many members.

With this Turnerian conclusion, I finished my talk and asked for questions and comments. A long silence was followed by several awkward interjections about minor ethnographic details, as most people in the room fidgeted nervously. Finally, Lazaro Mmala—a Muedan, a graduate of the elementary school at the Imbuho Catholic mission, a schoolteacher by training, a veteran of the Mozambican guerilla campaign for independence, and, now, an officer of the veterans association—cleared his throat and said, simply, "Andiliki, I think you misunderstand."

"How so?" I asked, trying to hide my anxiety.

"These lions that you talk about . . ." He paused, looking at me with what seemed a mixture of embarrassment and amusement. He then proceeded once more, cautiously but confidently, "they aren't symbols—they're real."[2]

A collective sigh enveloped the room. A lively discussion ensued to which nearly everyone present contributed accounts of incidents that they had experienced, or stories that they had heard, about lions stalking, attacking, and devouring people, as well as about the envious neighbors and kin who were to blame for these events. By the end of the session, I had collected nearly as much "data" about sorcery lions as I had gathered over the course of a year "in the field."

In Search of the Forward-Looking Peasant

When I first arrived in Mueda, I did not intend to make sorcery the focus of my research. I hoped, instead, to examine how Muedans envisioned the future. My research agenda was motivated by previous experience as a research assistant for a University of Wisconsin Land Tenure Center project assessing the breakup of the Mozambican state agricultural sector and the distribution of state farmland in the late 1980s and early 1990s (Myers and West 1993; West and Myers 1992, 1996).

Because state farms were strategically situated near waterways and transportation outlets, they were the focus of contentious claims when socialism collapsed in Mozambique. Former laborers/employees, as well as overseers/managers, of colonial plantations and/or the state farms that had displaced them staked claims to lands they had previously worked and, sometimes, even inhabited. People who had been evicted from these lands when colonial farmers initially occupied them—or their descendants—also asserted claims on the basis of ancestral domain. Further complicating the picture, refugees displaced by the sixteen-year-long Mozambican civil war had in some cases been "temporarily relocated" on these lands, and many expressed a desire to remain.

Once the war had ended, however, many in government sought to use these lands to attract postwar investment to Mozambique. Officials at various levels stood to benefit enormously from brokering such arrangements. To fend off claims to these lands made by ordinary Mozambicans, commercial interests and sympathetic state officials painted a portrait of "backward-looking" peasants—mired in traditional ways, disinterested in innovation or progress—who would underexploit these valuable resources. Based on Land Tenure Center research indicating that ordinary Mozambicans were inclined not only to produce for the marketplace but also to do so more efficiently, in many cases, than large commercial firms, we argued (pace Cramer and Pontara 1998) that these lands afforded opportunities for large numbers of Mozambicans to sustain themselves—opportunities not available to them elsewhere in the war-torn economy.

In subsequently elaborating an agenda for my dissertation research on the Mueda plateau, I sought directly to challenge the stereotype of the "backward-looking peasant" prevalent in Mozambique and elsewhere. In my research proposal, I posed the following question: How do rural Mozambicans envision their futures? I proposed to examine the practical and discursive strategies deployed by rural Mozambicans in their efforts to embrace, transform, or contest the official visions of the future with which they had been presented historically—whether under the rubric of colonial-era "community development," postindependence "socialist modernization," or postsocialist "liberalization" of the Mozambican polity and economy. I endeavored to examine not only how rural Mozambicans' strategies drew upon, and derived force from, local "tradition" but also how they constituted alternative designs for social transformation—how, in their own right, they articulated visions of the future.

In my quest to discover the "forward-looking Mozambican peasant," it made little sense, I thought, to examine beliefs and practices that were dismissed by many as superstition and that were often produced as evidence that rural Mozambicans stood outside the currents of modernity. Over the course of the preceding twenty years or so, anthropologists had largely turned away from such topics of research, asserting that the study of them generally exoticized the subjects of anthropological inquiry, rendering these people less comprehensible to, and thus disempowering them vis-à-vis, a Western audience.[1] While I remained wary of the contempt for others' ways of seeing the world manifest in such critiques,[2] I failed to see how the study of sorcery could do anything but undermine my research objectives.

During my first weeks on the Mueda plateau, I carried with me Martin Buber's *Paths in Utopia* (1949) and Lewis Mumford's *The Story of Utopias* (1922). Reading them at night, before I laid out my agenda for the next day of fieldwork, I cultivated my interest in understanding how people imagined a world not-yet-experienced. I asked myself, what resources did they draw upon to imagine a future? By what processes did they construct a future without merely reproducing or inverting the world that they knew and lived within? I reassured myself that rural Mozambicans sustained and articulated visions of the future as clearly and as forcefully as the Italian Futurists of whom I read.

By day, however, I grew frustrated in my attempts to tap the vein of Muedan futurism. When I asked those with whom I worked how they saw the future, they stared blankly at me. I took to asking how, when younger, they had envisioned the future, as well as how the present, in which they now lived, differed from that which they had once hoped for. Answers to my questions—when people understood them at all—were lifeless. Respondents merely compared their lives in the past to their lives in the present, pronouncing certain aspects better and others worse.

Finally, an elder named Lucas Ng'avanga responded directly to my search for the forward-looking peasant.

"I never thought of such things," he told me when I asked him how he imagined his life would be, in the future, when as a young man he joined the revolutionary nationalist movement.

"I lived my life from day to day. I didn't think about what was happening. I just did what I had to do. I didn't consider the future."

He may as well have added, "I am a backward-looking peasant!" And this from an active participant in the Mozambican *revolution!*

I sustained hope that the answers to my questions were not confirmation that Muedans looked only backward, but that they were, instead, evidence of methodological impasse. I wondered whether anyone could answer the questions that I posed, torn as they were from the context of life. I wondered to what extent visions of the future were, inevitably, intertwined with the present and the past—relatively minor, even insignificant, reworkings of the way one understood the world, simply, to be.

At the same time, I sought to find one or more "key informants" who, for whatever reason, possessed a rare capacity for reflection upon life as Muedans knew it. It was within this context that I first asked my Muedan research collaborators to identify *curandeiros* (Portuguese for "healers") with whom I might speak. The first *nkulaula* (Shimakonde for "healer") to whom I was introduced was an elderly man in the village of Matambalale named Kalamatatu. Mozambican socialism had been tolerant of neither anthropologists nor healers, casting the former as agents of a "colonial science" and the latter as purveyors of "obscurantism." As Mozambican socialism lingered forcefully in early "postsocialist" Mueda (a place long celebrated as the "cradle of the revolution"), I feared that any encounter between anthropologist and healer would be saturated with suspicion. I therefore tread lightly when introduced to Kalamatatu. He, however, spoke confidently and candidly. It was, in fact, he who broached the topic of sorcery, telling me that lion attacks were among the "misfortunes" that he treated, and explaining to me how he handled them: "When a lion is seen in the bush nearby, I prepare a pumpkin gourd with *ntela* [the generic term for any medicinal substance]. Then I go to the place where the lion was seen and I set fire to the bush. The fire will burn to where the lion is hiding. People follow the fire, discover the lion there, and kill it. The *ntela* prevents the lion from harming anyone." Kalamatatu also told me how he performed autopsies on slain lions, confirming that they were sorcery lions by finding *shidudu* (ground cassava leaves, eaten by Muedans as a relish) in their guts.[3]

Still, most Muedans remained reluctant in 1994 to participate in focused discussions with me about sorcery. Most references to sorcery were quick and vague. Sorcerers moved imperceptibly among us, Muedans sometimes reminded me, overhearing even our whispers, particularly when we spoke of them. It was best, I was often told, to avoid provoking such people whenever possible. Even healers, who confronted sorcerers daily as they treated the wounds produced by sorcery, generally spoke of these nemeses only in vague terms. Occasionally, they professed to me that it would be poor strategy to unnecessarily taunt and antagonize those with whom they did battle.

This is not to say that Muedans did not speak about sorcery. After the evening meal had been consumed, those with whom I lived and worked frequently huddled around the fire and, in hushed tones, told stories, or shared rumors, about sorcery's occurrence among them. Muedans, however, knew to contain sorcery discourse within prescribed bounds. It was not only sorcerers but also officials of the Mozambican Liberation Front (A Frente de Libertação de Moçambique, or FRELIMO) that they feared would overhear them.[4]

In this tense environment, I was party to frequent conversations about sorcery, so long as I listened quietly and asked only scattered questions. As soon as I expressed interest—as soon as I moved beyond simple expressions of revulsion or dread in response to what I heard and began to "interview" the tellers of these stories—conversations abruptly ended.[5]

Even so, as I spent time with Kalamatatu and a few others who spoke openly with me about the topic of sorcery, I became more attuned to the subtle, but frequent, references most Muedans made to sorcery during those evening sessions around the fire, and at other moments when they shared with one another what they knew of the illnesses and misfortunes of their neighbors and kin. These conversations often incorporated what, at first, seemed to me unrelated topics: the sound of an owl, at night, outside someone's house; the sudden appearance, in the middle of a pathway, of animal footprints; the perceived asymmetry of a sick person's face; the momentary resemblance of a corpse to a banana tree. In time, I myself learned to recognize the signs and symptoms of sorcery, at least in the images Muedans produced. Indeed, I slowly came to appreciate that sorcery constituted a language through which the Muedans with whom I worked comprehended and—even if euphemistically[6]—commented upon the workings of power in their midst. I slowly came to realize that if I was to discern how Muedans understood the social, political, and economic transformations they experienced—if I was to uncover their visions of changing times—I would have to learn the language of sorcery. As this would not be possible in the 1994 environment of postwar transition and electoral politicking, however, I set aside this component of my research agenda until a later date.

[handwritten margin note: needs to learn sorcery to understand Muedan's view of future]

"This Must Be Studied Scientifically"

After defending my doctoral dissertation in 1997 and taking up a visiting lectureship at the London School of Economics, I had the opportunity in 1999 to return to the Mueda plateau to undertake further intensive fieldwork. I determined this time to make sorcery the explicit focus of my research. I had been assisted in my fieldwork in 1994 by Marcos Agostinho Mandumbwe—a Muedan by origin, a FRELIMO veteran of the Mozambican independence war, an experienced field researcher who had worked at ARPAC for several years, and, at the time I met him, official historian at the Pemba office of the Association of Veterans of the War of National Liberation (Associação dos Combatentes de Luta de Libertação Nacional, or ACLLN). Our successful collaboration in 1994 had been founded upon shared interest in the history of the Mueda plateau region and, specifically, the history of the Mozambican independence war. While Marcos's status as a FRELIMO party cadre generally facilitated our work, I was unable to research politically sensitive topics—such as sorcery—in the company of such an active member of the ruling party. What research I did in 1994 on sorcery, I did with the assistance of ARPAC investigator Eusébio

Tissa Kairo, a younger man who had not been "trained by FRELIMO" and who, consequently, more easily followed his curiosity into the emergent spaces of Mozambican postsocialism. Because I had worked so well with Marcos on other issues, however, I hoped that he might be able to join me when I made sorcery the focus of my research in 1999. Much had changed, I knew, since we last worked together in Mueda. Mozambicans had had nearly five years' experience with democratic governance. While the governing FRELIMO party and the opposition, led by the Mozambican National Resistance (A Resistência Nacional Moçambicana, or RENAMO), squabbled endlessly in Parliament, their disagreements had not destroyed the new multiparty regime. Over the radio, Mozambicans daily heard voices criticizing FRELIMO policies, past and present. Those who spoke out, Mozambicans observed, were tolerated by the government. Many, indeed, thrived. What is more—I learned in my first few days in Pemba—topics like sorcery were openly discussed and debated, not only among ordinary people but also on state radio.

When I presented my sorcery-focused research agenda to Marcos, it met with his unqualified enthusiasm.

"This must be studied," he declared. "There is so much here to know, *mano* [brother]."

As he pondered the idea, his excitement grew deeper. "No one has ever studied these things in Mueda—not *scientifically*," he said. "But these things must be studied . . . *scientifically*."

Relieved by his enthusiasm, I did not ask what Marcos meant by studying sorcery "scientifically," but his words echoed both the Portuguese colonial emphasis on science as an "apolitical" endeavor (West 2004) and the FRELIMO celebration of "scientific socialism." As I later pondered what it might mean to study sorcery "scientifically," several questions presented themselves: In what kinds of situations did sorcery arise? What kinds of social relations engendered it? Who attacked whom, meaning, into what social categories did the perpetrators and victims generally fall? What motives and justifications were proffered for and attributed to sorcery attacks? To answer these questions, we would be required to catalogue Muedans' knowledge of sorcery; to systematically document as many events and perspectives as possible; to trace accusations and rumors of the practice of sorcery to their sources; and, ultimately, to ask questions that Muedans did not ask about sorcery.

A brief and unsubstantiated statement made by Yussuf Adam—a Mozambican researcher at the African Studies Center (Centro de Estudos Africanos, or CEA) at Eduardo Mondlane University (Universidade Eduardo Mondlane, or UEM)—served as a point of departure for the "scientific" study of sorcery as I imagined such an undertaking. In an article published in 1993 in the journal of the Mozambican Historical Archive (Arquivo Historico de Moçambique, or AHM), Adam asserted that those accused of producing lions in Mueda were "none other than landowners" (1993: 51–53). Adam's assertion echoed those of researchers working in Africa in the late colonial period who suggested that sorcery accusations ran along specific sociological lines of tension (Epstein 1967; Krige and Krige 1943; Marwick 1967; Wilson [1951] 1970).[1] Beidelman (1963: 74), for example, argued that, among Kaguru in Tanzania, the categories of people most often accused of sorcery included the economically successful and the politically powerful.[2] By contrast, Forde (1958: 170) suggested that among Yako, it was most often young women who were accused by members of the patrilineage into which they married. Begging the question of directionality, Terray (1975) suggested that accusations among Abron occurred most frequently between men and members of their fathers' matrilineages seeking to appropriate their wealth.[3]

Muedans, however, frustrated my every attempt to discern the sociological patterns of sorcery. The "data" that we gathered not only contradicted Adam's thesis but proved resistant to the formation of any coherent counterthesis. The more data we gathered, in fact, the more complicated became the sociology of Muedan sorcery.[4]

Muedans sometimes explicitly asserted that elders were indeed more generally suspected of the practice of sorcery than youths. In principle, because *mitela* (medicinal substances, used in the practice of sorcery and countersorcery) and their uses had to be learned, the longer one had to study, the more one might know. It followed, then, that sorcerers—particularly the most powerful among them—would be the aged. Indeed, Muedan villagers often accused the elderly among them of sorcery. When an elder's name was mentioned, Muedans would often exclaim, "Sheeeee! That old man knows something!"—a common euphemism for sorcery. The more physical infirmities an elder had, the more the passage of time had marked his body, the more suspect he became. A limp was considered a telltale sign that one had been injured in someone's yard at night by a *lipande* (antisorcery mine), set there by a countersorcerer to defend the occupant against sorcery attack.

It came as a surprise to me, then, when I discovered upon reading my field notes in the midst of my research that I had recorded more incidences of young people being accused of sorcery than of elders. Lucas Mwikumbi, in the village of Matambalale, told us that he suspected that most sorcery, these days, could in fact be attributed to village youths. "They have an advantage over elders," he explained to us. "They go from place to place very easily. Wherever they go, they can buy *mitela* and learn how to use them." Francisco Ntumbati, in the village of Matambalale, agreed with Mwikumbi. Today's young people, he told me, "run wild" in the villages, smoking *suruma* (cannabis) and finding outlets for their disrespect, including sorcery. In Nandimba, the healer Maurício Mpwapwele Moto told us, "Those who injure themselves [another euphemism for sorcerers] these days are children. They have no respect for their elders. Sometimes, these children will say to their elders, 'You cannot mess with me! If you do, I'll fix you!' Where there is such lack of respect, you can be sure that there is sorcery." In discussing sorcery and youth with us, the healer Vantila Shingini of Namande concluded, "Children these days play mean."

Just as Muedans generally stated, in principle, that elders had a comparative advantage over youth in learning the techniques of sorcery, so they concluded that men—who enjoyed greater mobility—had greater access to the requisite knowledge to perform sorcery than did women. Again, however, I discovered in my field notes that those with whom we had conversed more often attributed sorcery to women than to men when speaking concretely. Some flatly challenged the association of sorcery with men. Tiago Mateu of Matambalale told us, without hesitation, "Among sorcerers, there are more women than men!" Pikashi Lindalandolo told us that most of the sorcerers who came to him in need of treatment for injuries (a euphemism for having wounded oneself by tripping antisorcery defenses in the course of attacking someone) were in fact young girls.

My data also indicated that sorcery suspects were well distributed over other categorical divides in Muedan society. From the colonial era to the present, the poor accused their wealthier neighbors and kin of feeding insatiable appetites by preying upon their well-being. Whether as colonial-era labor migrants or as postcolonial entrepreneurs who combined the power of state office with command of the marketplace, the wealthy traveled widely, attracting suspicion that they had come to learn, and were able to deploy, novel sorcery techniques. "The 'big chiefs' eat everything!" Muedans often lamented. By the same token, these "big chiefs" suspected their poorer neighbors and kin of envy and accused them of seeking to devour their wealth through acts of sorcery. Whether labor migrants or politicians or businessmen who enjoyed success in postcolonial urban contexts, the relatively well-off articulated their suspicions most clearly by staying away from their villages of origin whenever possible.

Christians and non-Christians alike were also subject to sorcery accusations. The *humu* Mandia told us that Christians were the targets of sorcery because their wealth and knowledge of the Bible and of foreign languages attracted envy. So strong was the association of sorcery with non-Christians that Catholic missionaries at Nang'ololo had trouble keeping trainees, many of whom left the church's employ, missionaries told us, for fear that they would be "killed at night." Christians, on the other hand, were accused of practicing sorcery as well to protect themselves and their acquired wealth.

In light of all of this, I might simply have read my field notes as confirmation that sorcery provided an idiom for the expression of social tensions between Muedans of various categories and their respective sociological "others," were it not for the fact that my notes also bore evidence that Muedans suspected and accused those with whom they shared essential social attributes. In other words, men did not exempt other men from suspicion of sorcery, nor did women exempt other women. Youths accused youths, and elders accused elders. Accusations emerged not only across the divides between rich and poor, and between Christian and non-Christian, but also within these categories.

As my frustration peaked, the healer Atanásio Herneo of Matambalale explicitly stated what my data implicitly told me. When I asked him who sorcerers were—whether they were generally men or women, youths or elders, Christian or non-Christian, rich or poor—he answered bluntly, "Most people are *vavi* [sorcerers]—almost everyone. In fact, the person who is not a *mwavi* [sorcerer] is a rare person indeed."[5] The healer Boaventura Makuka told us much the same thing. When we asked him if there was any way to eliminate sorcery, he replied, "There are far more people in this world who are *vavi* than there are who are not. As long as there are people in the world, there will be *uwavi* [sorcery]!"

Sensing our "scientific" research agenda in peril, I turned to Marcos one evening. "We have been told that anyone can be a *mwavi*," I said. "But in the end, who are these *vavi*, generally, and who do they generally attack?" I heard my voice now pleading. "Is there some sort of pattern? Is there a *sense* to it all?!"

Marcos moved to the edge of the *igoli*[6] upon which he sat, resting his elbows on his knees and his face in his hands. He shook his head. When he looked up, he revealed a smile. "The trouble is, *mano,* you're trying to understand this thing *scientifically.* You can't understand this *scientifically.*"

"But you're the one who . . . !"—so befuddled was I that I found myself unable to finish my sentence.

"*Vavi* are *vavi,*" Marcos responded. "There is no *sense* to what they do." He threw his hands up in the air with gleeful exasperation. "They don't kill for wealth or power. They don't want money or tractors or airplanes."

"What *do* they want?" I asked.

"They crave human flesh. They can't get enough of it. That's what they want."

Marcos reminded me of what we had been told by Boaventura Makuka when we had asked him if a particular sorcerer—a man who, according to him, had made a lion to attack his own niece—had been motivated by envy (the "explanation" Muedans generally give for a sorcerer's attack). "He must have been," Makuka had answered, before adding, "although sometimes *vavi* attack because they decide that their victims have 'good meat on their bones'—just like you or I would say about a goat we decided to slaughter." Having invoked this image, Marcos now slumped back on the *igoli.* Following a pregnant pause, he looked at me and said, conclusively, "*That's uwavi.* You can't explain *that* scientifically!"

Belief as Metaphor

"There's no use trying," [Alice] said: "one ca'n't believe impossible things."
« LEWIS CARROLL, *Through the Looking-Glass* ([1871] 1998: 174) »

When I returned to the United States in 1995 after completion
of my dissertation fieldwork and told my anthropologist friends
and colleagues about sorcery lions, they seemed to know better
than to ask if I "believed in" such things. Which is not to say
that they knew—or even thought they knew—whether or not
I "believed"; rather, they avoided the question, it seemed to me,
because they considered any answer—mine *or* theirs—"problematic." Others with whom I shared accounts did not observe this
disciplinary taboo. When I started to teach in 1997, undergrad-
uate students asked with persistence if I "believed in" sorcery.
My answers were often witty, and always cagey. Embracing and
adapting Mark Rogers's idea that one can "believe a little bit"
(Rogers n.d.),[1] I often told people that I believed far more at
night—when the distant grunts and snorts of lions could, indeed, be heard from some of the villages in which I slept—than
I did in the light of day.

Muedans themselves sometimes asked me, in reference to
sorcery, "What do you think of all of this?" It seemed to me
that they expected me to dismiss "it all" as nonsense, as had

most Europeans they had known. When, during my first year in Mueda, Marcos asked me if I put stock in the power of the countersorcery "treatments" that we sometimes observed in healers' compounds, I answered, cautiously, that if others believed in these treatments, "there must be something to them." Clearly, I too found the question "problematic."

The question that I so assiduously avoided, however, stalked me from Mueda to the United States and the United Kingdom and back to Mueda again. In the dark of night, just outside the village of Diaca, as Marcos and I—in his nephew Nelito's dilapidated pickup truck—gathered speed to ascend the plateau on our journey from Pemba to begin our stint of intensive research on sorcery in 1999, a sleek silhouette appeared in the dim headlights before us less than thirty meters away. As quickly as we saw it, it slipped off the road and into the bush, its tail raised like a cobra poised to strike. So close were we that I could not bring the vehicle to a halt quickly enough to peer into the bush after the creature.

"*Shuvi* [leopard]?" I asked Marcos, "or *ntumi* [lion]?"

"I don't know," he immediately responded, adding, without taking a breath, "a lioness, I think."

As we completed the trip in eerie silence, I wondered to myself if we had "seen the same thing" before us in the dim headlights, despite my certainty that we somehow shared the adventure.[2]

So what *does* the anthropologist *make of it* when told that people *make*, or *make themselves into*, lions? In talking about sorcery lions as symbols five years earlier in the ARPAC seminar room, I had attempted to steer a course between two hazards arising from such questions. The first of these hazards was epitomized for me by Sister Rosa Carla, an Italian nun who founded and ran a health clinic in Mwambula, the village adjacent to the Nang'ololo mission to which she was assigned after the Mozambican civil war ended in 1992. The sister dedicated herself tirelessly to the clinic, dispensing much-needed and much-sought-after medications in recycled plastic 35 mm photographic film

[handwritten marginalia: believing in sorcery vs. us culture apperception]

canisters sent to her by friends and parishioners around the world. I respected her greatly and visited her from time to time. Once, when I was accompanied by Marcos and Tissa, she told me that she and her Toyota Hi-Lux had recently come upon a group of hunters from the village of Nshongwe who, only moments earlier, had killed a lion in the roadway. She obliged the villagers' request to help them transport the lion to the village center and, while doing so, got an earful of stories about lion-people. "It's all so unfortunate," she told me, glancing occasionally at Marcos and Tissa, whom she seemed to chastise as she spoke. "These *feiticeiros* [Portuguese for "sorcerers"] that they summon to come and kill these so-called lion-people—they are the same ones to whom my patients go for cures to infections and venereal diseases and malaria." Her voice was stern. "I treat people at my clinic in the morning, and they die at night in the *feiticeiro*'s house because they believe he can cure them. These *feiticeiros* do the most outrageous things. They poison people with their superstition." She shook her head as she lamented, "There is so much ignorance here. I can scarcely keep up with it all."[3]

To Sister Rosa Carla, I opposed in my mind Fernando Alves, a man of local legendry in Cabo Delgado. The son of mulatto parents, Alves lived in Pemba in the *bairro cimento* (the "concrete neighborhood," composed mostly of houses built by Portuguese occupants in the colonial period). While he earned a living as a self-employed mechanic, Alves was, like his father, an avid big-game hunter. When local hunters, armed with bows and arrows, were unable to dispense with lions that menaced villages anywhere in the province, Alves was summoned by the provincial government to kill them. Curiously, according to the Makonde trackers employed by Alves, he was adept at recovering *lyungo*, the life substance Makonde say a predatory animal, such as a lion, vomits in the moments immediately before dying. Alves indeed attributed his success as a hunter to his ability to find and ingest *lyungo*, as Makonde hunters have long sought to do. But Alves was not Makonde; nor was he from Mueda. Even

[handwritten margin notes: Sister Rosa Carla doesn't believe in lion sorcery, feiticeiros healing power; where and she develop this idea?; Fernando Alves; Alves mulatto - summoned to kill lions]

his African forebears were foreign to the region in which he hunted and to the Makonde "traditions" he invoked. His father's mother—a Ronga woman—came from as far away as Maputo, in the southernmost province of the country. In other contexts, he traced his hunter's pedigree to his Portuguese grandfather. Hearing of Alves's deeds, and occasionally listening to his stories, I found myself at times wondering how genuine his convictions were—whether this urban-born-and-raised man of mixed European-African descent had somehow "gone (more) native" or merely played on his guides' convictions to consolidate his status among them.

In any case, in the ARPAC seminar room, talking about sorcery lions, I felt myself awkwardly positioned somewhere between Sister Rosa Carla and Senhor Alves. Thoughts of the sister's dismissive words—ignorance, superstition—made me grimace. Thinking of Alves made me wonder if I had not detected sarcasm in Muedan accounts of him—indications that Muedans thought his claims as ridiculous as Sister Rosa Carla thought theirs.

Anthropologists have long searched for solid ground somewhere between the likes of Sister Rosa Carla and Senhor Alves—a position from which they might find sense in the worldviews of others without rendering their own views of the world nonsensical. E. E. Evans-Pritchard's classic work, *Witchcraft, Oracles and Magic among the Azande* ([1937] 1976), constituted a landmark in this disciplinary endeavor. Evans-Pritchard argued that the "strange beliefs" of Azande could not be dismissed as irrational. On the contrary, he asserted, Azande beliefs were internally coherent and worthy of serious ethnographic consideration (150). Even so, he ultimately concluded that Azande cosmology rested on the foundation of an errant assumption that witches existed in the first place. From the confident vantage point afforded him by the methods of scientific research, Evans-Pritchard stated that, although they were rational, Azande, quite simply, were wrong.[4] His conclusion echoed the assessment made of Trobri-

and Islanders' beliefs in magic by one of his professors, Broni-
slaw Malinowski: "subjectively true" but "objectively false" (in
Tambiah 1990: 81).[5]

Decades later, the anthropologist Paul Stoller would write,
"The Songhay world challenged the basic premises of my scientific training" (Stoller and Olkes 1987: 227). In his treatment of
Songhay sorcery, Stoller concluded, "Living in Songhay forced
me to confront the limitations of the Western philosophical
tradition" (227).[6] By contrast with Evans-Pritchard, Stoller determined, "For me, respect means accepting fully beliefs and
phenomena which our system of knowledge holds preposterous"
(229). Whereas the line dividing Evans-Pritchard from Sister
Rosa Carla is fine, the line between Stoller and Senhor Alves
may be finer. Stoller's claims to have been, during his time in
the field, not only the victim of sorcerers' attacks but also the
perpetrator were met with sarcastic derision from some of his
critics within the discipline (e.g., Beidelman 1989; cf. Baum
1990; Denzin 1990; Jackson 1988; Twitty 1987).[7]

As I spoke in the ARPAC seminar room, it seemed to me
that Victor Turner blazed a suitable trail between Sister Rosa
Carla and Senhor Alves. Turner's work contributed to the development of a "symbolist approach" that gained currency in
the discipline in the late 1960s (Morris 1987). Fundamental to
the symbolist approach is what Kenneth Burke referred to as a
shift away from treating "magical beliefs" as "bad science" and
toward treating them as a form of "rhetorical art" (Burke 1969).
John Beattie, in his discussion of the study of ritual, elaborated
on this approach, proclaiming:

> I ally myself squarely . . . with those who assert that ritual is essen-
> tially expressive and symbolic, and that it is this that distinguishes
> it from other aspects of human behaviour, and that gives rise to its
> characteristic problems. In this respect it is allied with art rather
> than with science, and it is susceptible of similar kinds of under-
> standing. When we contemplate a work of art, we do not usually
> ask what use it is (although of course we may do so); we ask rather

rituals as art, not science

*art + ritual
both contains
meaning*

what it means, what are the ideas and values which it is intended
to express? Like art, ritual is a kind of language, a way of saying
things. (1966: 65)[8]

Considering that Victor Turner defined a symbol as "a thing
regarded by general consent as naturally typifying or representing or recalling something by possession of *analogous qualities* or
by association in fact or in thought" (1967: 19, emphasis added),
it comes as no surprise that anthropologists adopting the symbolist approach have sometimes conceived of their informants'
beliefs as *metaphors*. Take, for example, the work of Jean Comaroff (1985) on Zionist healing cults in South Africa. Comaroff
has argued that the physical afflictions suffered by individual
Tshidi served, when she conducted her fieldwork among them,
as metaphors for the larger "ills" of apartheid society. "The metaphors of social contradiction deployed by these cults," she has
written, "are often rooted in the notion of the body at war with
itself, or with its immediate social and material context; and de-
sired transformations focus upon 'healing' as a mode of repair-
ing the tormented body and, through it, the oppressive social
order itself" (9). More recently, Luise White has advanced a
similar argument in her historical work on the widespread belief in colonial Africa in vampire-firemen (*wazimamoto*) who
sucked the blood of captured victims: "I think there are many
obvious reasons why Africans might have thought that colonial
powers took precious substances from African bodies . . . I think
bloodsucking by public employees is a fairly obvious *metaphor*
for state-sponsored extractions" (2000: 18, emphasis added).[9]
Even more apropos to Muedan sorcery lions, Michael Jackson has asserted that "*suwa'ye* ["witchcraft" in the language of
Karanko in Sierra Leone, among whom he worked] is a common metaphor for extraordinary powers" (1989: 91). "Beliefs,"
Jackson has concluded, "are more like metaphors than many
dare imagine" (66).[10]

In treating beliefs as metaphors, it would seem that Comaroff, White, Jackson, and many others have escaped the dilemma

posed by assessing their scientific validity. They have suggested that these beliefs constitute alternative ways of talking about historical events and social realities. As White has phrased it, they "look for what such beliefs articulate in a given time and space" (2000: 44). These expressions, they have told us, might best be understood as richly creative languages (to use Beattie's terminology) with which to talk about reality—languages that inflect and refract others, including the language of science, but that need not be seen as contradicting science.[11]

In this vein, I suggested to my audience in the ARPAC seminar room that lions served Muedans as symbols with which to think about and speak about the complexities and contradictions of power. Sorcery lions, I suggested, served Muedans as metaphors for social predation, whereas the lions that resided in the bodies of *vahumu* served as metaphors for regal power. I neither dismissed nor adopted Muedans' way of talking about these lions; I pronounced them neither true nor false.[12] Even so, Lazaro Mmala protested. In so many words, he told me, "Andiliki, metaphors don't kill the neighbors, lion-people do!"[13]

"The Problem May Lie There"

"I could tell you my adventures—beginning from this morning," said Alice a little timidly; "but it's no use going back to yesterday, because I was a different person then."

"Explain all that," said the Mock Turtle.

"No, no! The adventures first," said the Gryphon in an impatient tone: "explanations take such a dreadful time."

« LEWIS CARROLL, *Alice's Adventures in Wonderland* ([1865] 1998: 91) »

On 15 June 1994, Marcos and I traveled from the town of Mueda, where we were then staying with one of Marcos's *likola* sisters,[1] to the village of Nanenda on the eastern edge of the plateau. Our objective for the day was to identify and interview elders who had witnessed the Portuguese assault on the plateau (ca. 1917) that had culminated in the colonial "pacification" of the Makonde people. We were accompanied on our excursion by Marcos's brother-in-law, Joseph Mery, who took advantage of the opportunity our trip afforded him to purchase a pig at "village price" and to transport it back to the town of Mueda, where he would butcher it and sell roasted bits of pork to those gathered there the following day to mark the thirty-fourth anniversary of the Mueda Massacre.[2]

Mery's negotiations outlasted our interviews. As we waited for him, I felt unusually tired. My body ached more acutely than it normally did after a day spent perched precariously on a sagging *igoli*. I considered intruding upon Mery's negotiations and paying the asking price for the pig myself, but decided better of it. Finally, a price was agreed upon, and we headed for Mueda with a squealing pig in the back of our pickup and my head pounding.

I turned in before the evening meal as Mery busied himself clearing out his chicken coop to house the agitated pig. Despite the noise, I fell fast asleep before the sun had set. Around ten o'clock at night, I awoke with a jolt, my body seized with chills. I trembled uncontrollably beneath the covers. Realizing that something was gravely wrong, I sat up to call for Marcos, who lay sleeping a few meters away. As the night air rushed in beneath the covers, I convulsed violently. Frightened by the apparent vulnerability of my body to the world around me, I recoiled, gathering the covers close. I knew that I could not sleep—that I urgently needed something other than sleep. I convinced myself that I could, with a little courage, tolerate the air and, again, rose to call for Marcos, but the cold was more intolerable than I imagined possible. Overpowered completely by the elements in which I was suspended, I retreated, shivering, into fetal position. I felt as though I would shake myself to pieces. I feared, somehow, that I would dissolve into the world that surrounded me. For more than half an hour, I called to Marcos, my summonses muffled by my own shivering and by the blankets I desperately clenched.

Finally, Marcos awoke. Before I knew what was happening, I felt my bare feet touching the damp ground. On the path to the pit latrine, something broke loose deep inside me, erupting through my chest and out of my mouth. I collapsed. Marcos wrapped his arms around me from behind and, once again, I found myself moving. My legs dangled numbly. I felt another eruption from within, this time flowing beneath me. I was unable to differentiate myself from that which burst out from within me. I became uncontrollable flows of lava. Then, for a moment, my body was solid once more. I rediscovered my arms and legs, and the back of my neck. A surge of heat passed through me. The cool night air soothed me, and I wanted to sleep. Marcos helped clean me up and lay me down in his bed (closer to the latrine). He sat by my side as I rested. My respite, however, soon expired. I was overwhelmed, again, by a sense of urgency, a sense of disintegration, a sense of doom. Again and again, throughout the night, my body met with overpowering forces from within and opened itself to flow into a hostile world, leaving me more exhausted, each time, than I had ever felt before.

By night's end, I had found sleep, but I was reawakened by the first rays of sunlight. My eyes ached deeply. I heard voices and scuffling, smelled dust in my nostrils, and then heard the screams of Mery's pig, at first full-throated but, in time, gurgling with blood. It seemed to me that the animal was forever suspended in the throes of death—that it could escape neither the butcher's hands nor life itself.

When I next awoke, the sun was high in the sky. It burned me as if from within my body. Sitting beside me, Marcos looked at me with grave concern. I shared his anxiety. For the first time in hours, I was alive enough to fear that I might die. As Marcos could not drive a stick shift, he placed me in the driver's seat of the pickup. We drove to the United Nations command post, where government troops were then quartered, awaiting demobilization.[3] I requested passage on one of the daily UN helicopter flights between Mueda and Pemba but was denied. An Italian logistics officer at the camp—whom everyone called "Orso" ("bear" in Portuguese)—took pity on me, lending me his bed and asking the camp doctor to look in on me. The doctor did not have the resources with which to test me for malaria or intestinal parasites, but he gave me Fansadar and Flagyl nonetheless. Orso showed me how to fire the AK-47 that he subsequently slipped under the bed. "We've had some trouble here lately," he said, referring to incidents in which troops had taken him hostage and issued demands for larger rations and other handouts. As I slipped off to sleep, I wondered how a loaded weapon under my bed could bring me anything but trouble.

I awoke every few hours to an audience of more than 100 *mapiko* masks that Orso had collected during his stay on the plateau. While sitting with me, Marcos and Mery identified several of the masks as ones used in initiation rites in specific Muedan villages in specific years. Several times a day, young men poked their heads into the tent, holding yet another mask in their hands and—confusing me for Orso—asking if I wanted to buy it. When Orso was there, he would analyze the mask and point out its "imperfections," but he would buy it nonetheless, turning to me and saying, "I don't want to offend." When he asked if I knew of any university in the United States that had a museum that might be interested in buying the masks from him, I told him I did not. As I faded in and out of hallucinatory states, I wondered whether or not I was, in fact, Orso and, if not, how my work differed from his crass acquisition of Makonde artifacts.

On the third day, with arms draped over Marcos's and Mery's shoulders, I fled the camp and took refuge with a family of British Bible translators living in Mueda town. Dysentery persisted for a week, but a steady diet of Earl Grey tea and bland foods and the attentive care of people who spoke my mother tongue allowed me to gather strength. I eventually drove Marcos and myself off the plateau and back to Pemba, where I caught the next flight to Maputo. In twelve days, I had lost twenty-seven pounds.

Exactly two weeks later, I boarded a plane returning to Pemba. The Mozambican doctor at the U.S. embassy clinic suspected that I had had shigella, malaria, or possibly both. Having regained only two or three pounds, I was not yet ready, physically, to return to Mueda. I knew, however, that if I did not soon return to the plateau, I might never complete my fieldwork. When I fell ill, one of my greatest fears had been realized, but this fear was only one among many that defined my fieldwork experience. Convalescing in Maputo, my fears grew into obsessions with potential menaces awaiting me in Mueda—fatal vehicular accidents; financially or logistically debilitating vehicular breakdowns; encounters with spiders, snakes, leopards, or lions; landmines (from either the independence war or the civil war); demobilized-troops-turned-armed-bandits; suspicious government officials (who might, for example, deny me access to my field site); extortionist police officers (who might confiscate my vehicle on the pretense that it was stolen);[4] encounters with hostile, drunken villagers; cerebral malaria; and so on, ad infinitum. Only by placing myself once more in the field, I knew, could I displace these imagined perils with an existence devoid of their realization.

Within days of my return to Pemba, Marcos and I set off together for Mueda. Seeing the expressions on the faces of people astonished by my rapid return—or by my return altogether—filled me with disorientation but, also, with an exhilarating sense of madness. While I was in this state of mind, Marcos said to me, "*Bwana,* let's go see Humu Mandia." I protested that travel to the *humu's* village of Nimu was not on our agenda—that it was, in fact, well out of our way—but when Marcos insisted, I relented despite not understanding the motive for his unusual rigidity.

When we arrived at Mandia's compound, we were warmly received. Although we had met Mandia once before in Mueda, we had never had the opportunity to converse with him. Now, we sat quietly in the dark interior of the *humu's* house. The frailty of Mandia's voice somehow accentuated the strength of his words. To my surprise, Marcos uncharacteristically (for that time, in 1994) began to ask him questions about sorcery, about his role in combating its destructive consequences in Makonde society, and about the forms of treatment he undertook to protect and cure those who came to him. I was quickly drawn into the fascinating conversation that developed between the two of them, revealing as it did the *humu's* ambivalent relationship with lions, whose meat he had ritually ingested but with whom, as a "brother," he had "no contradictions."

Somewhat against the grain of my anthropological interests, Marcos steered Mandia away from such abstractions, however, and toward the discussion of specific ailments and their cures. Suddenly, I realized that the subject of Marcos's interest was *my* ailment and *my* cure.

"Have you had conflictual relations with anyone lately?" Mandia asked me. The question's syntax reminded me of a health clinic worker interviewing a patient who presented with a sexually transmitted disease, while its semantics conjured for me the image of a homicide detective interrogating members of a victim's family. Unsure of the sort of conflictual relations Mandia had in mind—unsure of how to go about asking myself the question, much less answering it—I looked to Marcos.

Marcos raised his eyebrows and turned his head downward slightly before meeting my eyes once more. "There was that incident in Namaua," he said to me in Portuguese.

I nodded in affirmation but remained uncertain, still, how to respond to Mandia.

Marcos spoke for me: "A few days before he fell ill, there was an argument with someone."

Marcos and I had traveled to Namaua to conduct research there for the first time. As was our practice, we had presented ourselves to the village president, explained our agenda, shown our "credentials" (including a letter of introduction from the district administrator), and requested permission to conduct interviews. The village president had welcomed us to work in his village, but as we sat conversing with him, we were approached by the president of the locality that encompassed Namaua and a few smaller villages. We quickly surmised that he was drunk. He asked what we were doing in Namaua, and when we told him, he declared that we would not under any circumstances work in one of *his* villages. Marcos spoke calmly and respectfully to the official and showed him our credentials, but the locality president only grew more agitated. Marcos decided it best that we leave before the encounter turned violent, and I followed his lead.

"Was the argument resolved peacefully?" Mandia now asked Marcos.

Marcos let loose a snort of laughter. "No one was injured. But the situation was only resolved after the authorities intervened."

My mind raced back to the conversation that Marcos and I had had as we traveled back to Mueda after being "evicted" from Namaua. Tensions were high at the time, as Muedans prepared for the 1994 elections, and in accordance with the mandate of the ruling FRELIMO party, villagers remained "vigilant" vis-à-vis unfamiliar visitors who might be working in collaboration with the political opposition. Tensions in Namaua were exacerbated by the fact that the village was "home" to the head of the Mozambican military, Brigadier Ladis "Lagos" Lidimo, whose reputation for ruthlessness was as great among the villagers who tended to his local affairs and protected his interests in the region as it had been in the liberated zones he had policed as a security agent during the independence war or among the troops he commanded, or fought against, during the civil war. Understandably, the locality president wished to avoid the introduction of new variables into the complex political environment over which he was expected to preside, and hoped that Marcos and I could be made to disappear. Marcos, however, knew that word would spread that we had been chased from Namaua. If we did not assert our right to work there—if we did not reestablish the legitimacy of our project—authorities in other villages might follow suit, banning us from work in their villages as well. We therefore drove directly from Namaua to the office of the Mueda district administrator to report that, notwithstanding the administrator's letter of introduction, we had been denied access to one of *his* villages. The administrator had immediately dispatched a messenger to summon the locality president to Mueda town, whereupon the official was "disciplined" and instructed not to interfere with our work in the future.

"Hmmm," Mandia said, looking me in the eyes.

Marcos turned to me and said, "The problem may lie there."

As I sat wondering how I had arrived at this moment—how I had come to be sitting in a dank hut searching my recent experiences for signs of sorcery, and how I felt about Marcos having brought me there—Marcos asked Mandia to show him some of the *mitela* of which he had spoken earlier in the conversation. Mandia focused his scrutinizing gaze upon Marcos—and then me—for some time. Then, without a word, he rose and entered into a small area set off from the rest of the house's interior. He reemerged with a small animal-skin bag from which he unpacked various containers filled with ground leaves, powders, and fluids. Based upon the preceding conversation, he chose two substances. The first was a white powder called *ing'opedi*. He explained to us that the first act undertaken by a newly installed *humu* was to go from house to house treating the inhabitants who fell under his protective jurisdiction with *ing'opedi*. He placed his right thumb over the opening of the small bottle containing an ivory-white powder and turned it upside down. He pressed his thumb gently to Marcos's forehead, painting a vertical line and then a horizontal one. I wondered if the manner in which he anointed Marcos with *ing'opedi* had been affected by Christian rites, for it was a cross he painted on Marcos's forehead.[5] He turned to me and asked if I wished to be treated. I said quietly that I did, and placed myself before him. Mandia told me that as I moved about on the plateau with objects of value—my truck, my camera, my tape recorder and, even, my "project" itself—I inevitably attracted attention and envy. I was, therefore, in need of protection. After he treated me, he explained to us that the substance was made of *mapira* (sorghum) flour mixed with certain kinds of *mitela*. It would soon disappear, he told us, but the protection it afforded would linger. Apparently, sorcerers would see the mark for some time and know that, should they attack us, they would have Mandia to contend with.

The second substance Mandia did not name, but he explained that it was made of other forms of *mitela* mixed with bee honey. He took a short stick and dipped it into the bottle containing the nameless substance. He then placed the end on his own tongue, closed his lips around it, and pulled it out of his mouth while spinning it. He then did this with Marcos and, finally, with me. This treatment, he explained, gave us force that would

[handwritten margin note: Mandia puts protector on Marcos + narrator]

serve in fighting off illness. He looked at me, smiled gently, and said that I also needed this.

Days after we had visited Mandia, Marcos orchestrated a meeting with Kalamatatu as well, whom he also persuaded to treat us. Of Kalamatatu, Marcos requested *lukulungu lwa ntumi*—the throat meat of a slain lion, administered to ensure that its recipient's voice was respected by all who heard him speak.

Whose Metaphors?

It was only weeks after falling ill—and being treated—that I addressed my colleagues at ARPAC. In speaking about lions as complex symbols, I sought not only to make sense of the ethnographic data I had been given by Kalamatatu, Mandia, and others but also to make sense of my own experiences of illness and recovery. In the sense I made of *uwavi* (sorcery), *kulaula* (healing), and *vantumi va nkaja* (sorcery lions), however, my audience heard nonsense.

Andras Sandor has suggested that, notwithstanding good intentions, anthropologists deploying the symbolist approach "[assimilate] other people's 'facts' to [their] idea of 'meaningful fiction'" (1986: 102).[1] Luise White has warned that metaphor is often interpreted as a "polite academic term for false" (2000: 42).[2] Why might this be so? To appreciate why Lazaro Mmala took my assertion that sorcery lions were symbols (or metaphors) as a statement that they were not "real," we must, I subsequently came to think, more closely examine how metaphor is defined, how it works, and to what ends it may be used.

James Fernandez has written, "However men may analyze their experiences in any domain, they inevitably know and understand them best by referring them to other domains for elucidation" (1972: 58). Through metaphoric reference, according to Fernandez, people suggest that "something much more concrete and graspable—a rolling stone, a bird in the hand—is equivalent to the essential elements in another situation we have difficulty grasping" (43–44). Through such "predication upon an inchoate situation" (43), Fernandez has suggested, people are able to clarify an otherwise incomprehensible world.

The essential point here is that metaphor refers people to a semantic domain that is *separate* from the one they seek to understand. The most celebrated examples of metaphor are ones in which it is clear to all concerned—speaker and listeners—that the metaphoric predicate and the subject to which it is applied inhabit *distinct* domains. An active person is not *actually a roll-*ing stone, nor is an immediate opportunity *actually* a bird in a hand. Such metaphors work, David Sapir has explained, by making us "aware of the simultaneous likeness *and unlikeness* of the two terms" (1977: 9, emphasis added)[3] and then asking us to imagine, *knowing it to be untrue,* that the two terms are alike in more ways than immediately apparent. The case he used to illustrate his point is delightfully convenient. The assertion that "George is a lion," he has written, "allows us . . . to assume for a moment that although George is 'really' like a lion only in certain specific ways [both are mammals, for example], he might be a lot more like a lion than in just those ways [for example, George is fierce]" (9). According to Sapir, the metaphor works not only because it links two separate semantic domains—the animal kingdom and George's social milieu—but also because it calls attention to the chasm between the domains that it bridges. George's lion-like fierceness makes him an *unusual* human *because* humans, after all, are not *really* animals. "Metaphor," Sandor has said, in support of Sapir's point, "cannot come about unless it is reflected upon" in this way (1986: 113).

So what, then, *is* to be made of the statement, proffered in a Muedan village, that a fellow—call him Imbwambwe—periodically transformed himself into a lion and menaced his neighbors? Imbwambwe—and, more importantly, the lion that he

became—inhabited the *same* domain as Imbwambwe's neighbors. As Lazaro Mmala reminded me, the lion, Imbwambwe,
bared teeth and claws with which he drew blood and tore the
flesh of his victims.[4] His "reality" to them—his copresence in
their ontological domain—was a matter of life and death, for he
left in his wake mauled bodies and terrorized witnesses.[5] When
neighbors saw Imbwambwe, the lion, in the village, they took
refuge inside their homes. Once a countersorcerer was summoned to provide the requisite medicinal substances to protect
them and to render the lion vulnerable, they hunted it down
with bow and arrow. Their success in the hunt meant that Imbwambwe, the man, would die. Failing in the hunt, they may
have directly sought out Imbwambwe, the man, and lynched
him. In any case, if, when they spoke of Imbwambwe, the lion,
Muedans did not think themselves to be making reference to
a separate and distinct domain to express something about the
character and behavior of Imbwambwe, the man (if they did
not consider themselves to be "predicating upon an inchoate
subject" but, instead, to be describing a "*real* and present dan-
ger"), can we call Imbwambwe, the lion, a metaphor?[6]

Beattie himself posed the question, "[I]n what sense, if any,
can we say that people's institutionalized behaviour is symbolic
if, as may well be the case, they themselves do not seem to know
[here, I would substitute "do not think"] that it is?" (1966: 66).[7]
According to Sandor, "no metaphor occurs where none is recognized" (1986: 103).[8] Yet Turner would not let us be dissuaded.
In the essay that I shared with my ARPAC colleagues, Turner
posed a similar question: "[I]f Ndembu do not recognize the
discrepancy between their interpretation of the milk tree symbolism and their behavior in connection with it, does this mean
that the discrepancy has no relevance for the social anthropologist?" (1967: 26). Answering his own query, Turner confidently
asserted, "Here the important question must be asked, 'meaning for whom?'" (25–26); in other words, he suggested, symbols
may lie not in the eyes of their producers but, instead, in the
eyes of their anthropologist beholders.[9]

Still, Turner's logic (not lost on Lazaro Mmala) left me in a different place than I had intended when I entered the seminar room at ARPAC. For, in the end, Turner's position, as applied to my case—that Muedans failed to recognize their own symbols (or metaphors); that they mistook allegories for identities (a charge, incidentally, commonly leveled against conspiracy theorists; see Sanders and West 2003)—had me asserting, with echoes of colonial condescension, that Muedans' deceived themselves; had me arguing, in the tone of revolutionary socialism, that their understanding of the world in which they lived was a form of "false consciousness."

Powers of Perspective
and Persuasion

According to plan, in the dry season of 1999, Marcos and I conducted research in villages we knew well, but we focused, this time, on healers and healing practices, including, of course, countersorcery. Midway through our research, as previously arranged, we were joined by Tissa. Together, we spent time with more than a hundred different healers, ultimately concentrating on the dozen or so with whom we were best able to work.

Ironically, while the Mozambican state now demonstrated greater official tolerance for traditional healers and—backed by foreign researchers and nongovernmental organizations (NGOs)—even *celebrated* "traditional healing" in some contexts, healers themselves enthusiastically embraced emergent opportunities to incorporate new techniques into their healing repertoires. The eclecticism of Muedan healers challenged the definitional boundaries of "traditional healing" in myriad ways (West and Luedke 2005). Whereas some healers adopted "modern" or "official" healing methods or both, others borrowed "traditions" from other times and places. Some, it seemed, invented healing "traditions" from scratch (West 2005b).

[handwritten marginal note:] N60's embracing traditional healing in western realm

One healer, in particular, frustrated my attempts to understand by what criteria Muedans themselves judged the legitimacy of a healer's practice. In the village of Namande, Julia Nkataje healed her clients by scribbling indecipherable figures on bits of paper, boiling the paper in water, and offering the water to her patients to drink three times daily (West 2005b). "Voices" instructed her to write, she told us, and while her scribblings "meant something," she admitted that *she* "did not know what." Although Julia herself had once been healed by a Muslim man who tore pages from the Koran, rolled them up, and placed them in a bottle for patients to carry with them, she professed to be a Christian; indeed, she proudly told us, the Virgin Mary had appeared to her four times.

In the evening after our first meeting with Julia, Marcos and I found Tissa where we had left him earlier in the day, in the compound of Marcos's Matambalale relatives. He was seated in the open air, warming himself as best he could in occasional bursts of sun beneath a cloudy sky. He had been suffering for days from intermittent fevers and chills. He had diagnosed himself with malaria and had persuaded someone at the hospital in Mueda to validate his assessment with a prescription for chloroquine.

"It will pass," he assured me. Referring back to my own bout with malaria, he added, grinning broadly, "We Africans are more resistant to malaria than you *vajungu* [foreigners]."

A basin full of oranges sat on the ground by his side. He asked for my Swiss Army knife, casting away the dull wooden-handled knife that he had previously been using. He asked us what we had learned in Namande.

Marcos laughed. "We learned how to boil words!" he said.

"Ahhhhh. You were with that woman there who heals with her own kind of holy water," Tissa quickly surmised.

"That's the one."

"Nkataje?"

"Yes," I answered. "How did you know?"

Tissa hesitated slightly. "She's well known. Didn't you see how many people were there? There were lots of people there, weren't there?"

"It's a healing factory!" Marcos replied.

We sat for a few minutes before Tissa broke the silence. "So what did you think of it, Andiliki?" I interpreted his laughter to mean that he found humor in his memories of Julia's compound.

I gathered my thoughts for a moment, trying to figure out how to respond with anthropological sensitivity in the face of the skepticism that I thought I detected in Marcos's and Tissa's remarks.

"I don't know what to think of her," I said. "It doesn't seem to me that she's really an *nkulaula* [healer]."

Tissa worked my knife around and around the orange in his hand, creating a spiraling rind that coiled in a pile on the ground beneath him. "Why?" he asked.

"It seems to me that she has just made the whole thing up," I said. "I mean, she scribbles on paper, boils it in water, and has people drink it. Malaria, tuberculosis, broken bones, sore throats, sorcery, AIDS . . . it's all the same to her . . . just drink the water."

[handwritten margin note: writing on paper + boiling]

"You saw all the people in her compound, didn't you?" Tissa responded.

"Look," I said, "every other *nkulaula* that we have talked with uses *mitela* made from leaves, roots, tree bark, or animal parts. Some have special kinds of *mitela* that they discovered themselves. But there are many kinds of *mitela* that all *vakulaula* [healers] know. Masters pass this knowledge on to their apprentices, or ancestors pass it on to the descendants they possess."

I suddenly realized that I was arguing, against the grain of my anthropological predilections, in favor of recognizing the "legitimacy" only of *kulaula* (healing) orthopraxis (whatever *that* was). I carried on, nonetheless, trying to convince myself along the way that I was merely playing devil's advocate.[1]

"In any case, there is a certain 'tradition' to healing, isn't there? You can't just ignore all of this and still be an *nkulaula*, can you? I mean, would other *vakulaula* recognize Julia Nkataje as an *nkulaula*? She doesn't know even the most common forms of *mitela*. She has no *mitela*!"

"What about the water she uses?" Marcos asked. "That's her *mitela*."

I shrugged my shoulders. "Water. Just water. Water for everyone, no matter what ails them." I shook my head. "Where's the *knowledge* in that? Anyone can do that."

"It has to do with the verses she writes that she puts in the water," Tissa answered.

"Who taught her that? What sense does it have? *She* doesn't even know!" I turned to Marcos. "We asked her, didn't we?" Marcos nodded. "She said she didn't *know* what her figures mean. She's illiterate. She just scribbles on paper. That's not *kulaula*!"

"But it works!" Tissa answered. "Look at all the people who go to her. She must know *something*, because she heals them." Suddenly, the touch of sarcasm was gone from his voice.

"Tissa," I said, "she told us that she could heal infections. We asked her how long it took. She said that sometimes it takes only days, but sometimes it takes as long as six months. Six months! In six months, the body can heal itself of an infection. It has nothing to do with the healer. With all those sick people in her yard all the time, there are bound to be people who get better. I don't see where she has anything to do with it."

"That woman *knows something*," Tissa responded, simply. With a mixture of defiance and shame, he admitted, finally, that he had been treated by Nkataje three years earlier. She had cured him of recurrent headaches, he told us.

The pile of orange peels at his feet was now substantial. I thought of how pleased my mother would have been that he had consumed nearly a dozen. She has infinite faith in vitamin C, my mother, and I was sure that she would see a place for it in the treatment of malaria.

We sat quietly for a few moments. I then asked them both, "Isn't it possible that an *nkulaula* can be a fraud?" I reached for one of the orange peels. "I'm not an *nkulaula*," I said. "But what's to prevent me from squeezing the juice out of a dozen oranges into this basin and telling Tissa, 'Okay, soak your feet in this orange juice. This is my *mitela*. It will cure your malaria.' Tissa told me himself that he will survive this bout with malaria. He told me that Africans are more resistant than *vajungu*. We know he's going to get better. But if I get him to soak his feet in my orange juice, I can claim that I cured him, can't I?"

We all laughed together.

"I'm going to try that," Marcos said. "I'll be the most famous *nkulaula* in Cabo Delgado. And I'll tell everyone that I learned my *mitela* from a powerful *njungu!*" He reached out to clasp my hand as we continued laughing.

Tissa then punctuated our laughter to set the record straight: "But your orange juice wouldn't heal me."

"I don't see how Julia Nkataje's water is any different," I said.

Marcos now became serious as well. "*Mano,* the important thing is that people *believe* in it. You know that your orange juice is just orange juice, so no one will *believe* you. Julia Nkataje *believes* in her cure, so her patients do too. If a person *believes* they are cured, they will be cured."

Marcos told a story to illustrate his argument. "I once healed a woman. She was trembling the way people do when they are possessed. I'm no *nkulaula,* and I don't have any *mitela.* So I took ordinary water and 'anointed' her with it, the way Humu Mandia does with *ing'opedi.*" He reached forward and rubbed his thumb on my forehead in the sign of a cross. "I told her to go to sleep. When she woke up, I told her to go and bathe."

"Did it work?" I asked.

Marcos smiled broadly. "She got better."

"But did you *heal* her?" I asked.

Marcos continued to smile but remained silent, leaving open to interpretation whether he was himself persuaded of his

[handwritten margin note:] in people believe in boiled water cures come from belief

healing powers and whether he considered as "real" the healing "power of persuasion."

In any case, I remembered my own experience as the beneficiary of Mandia's and Kalamatatu's healing treatments. These treatments had indeed *worked* for me, in more ways than one. Both Mandia and Kalamatatu had instructed Marcos and me to keep our treatment secret lest word of it make us targets for sorcerers attempting to prove their capacities to overcome such treatments. Nonetheless, within hours of our sessions, I caught Marcos—and even our healers themselves—speaking in hushed tones with acquaintances about our having been treated. "Don't tell anyone, but Andiliki has been treated." These people, in turn, told others; "Don't tell anyone, but . . ."

Word spread quickly and soon, it seemed, everyone knew. Later, Marcos commented to me that this spreading of the news actually benefited us: people (including potential sorcerers) found out about the treatment, he explained, and then "respected" its recipients for fear of the medicinal specialist who had healed them.[2] In this way, Mandia and Kalamatatu made my illness and recovery a meaningful event to Muedans, thereby producing tangible social effects. Indeed, knowing that others knew I had been treated, I had the sense that I was afforded more "respect." My anxieties diminished accordingly.

What is more, Mandia and Kalamatatu made my experience comprehensible, *in Muedan terms,* to me—effectively redefining the world around me. As they defined for me a role that made sense to Muedans, I began to experience Mueda differently than before. To be sure, I had collected valuable "data" as Mandia's and Kalamatatu's patient. But now, instead of trying to "get things into perspective" by finding a place from which to observe the Muedan social landscape—including the terrain of sorcery—*from the outside,* as Jackson (1989: 8) has put it, I found myself trying to comprehend and engage with the Muedan world of sorcery from a perspectival space *within* it created for me by my own *vakulaula*.[3]

[margin handwritten note:] "being treated" demands respect

Making Meaning,
Making the World

What then is truth? A mobile army of metaphors, metonyms and anthropomorphisms—in short a sum of human relations, which have been enhanced, transposed and embellished poetically and rhetorically, and which after long use seem firm, canonical and obligatory to a people: truths are illusions about which one has forgotten that this is what they are; metaphors which are worn out and without sensuous power; coins which have lost their pictures and now matter only as metal, no longer as coins.
« FRIEDRICH NIETZSCHE, "On Truth and Lie in an Extra-moral Sense" (1976: 46–47) »

Dreams are true while they last, and do we not live in dreams?
« ALFRED TENNYSON, *The Higher Pantheism*, line 4 »

According to Émile Durkheim (to whom "symbolist" anthropologists trace their roots), religion is essentially symbolic (Morris 1987: 119). "God is only a figurative expression of . . . society," Durkheim wrote ([1915] 1964: 226); elsewhere he called religion a metaphor for the social group (Morris 1987: 119–120).[1] On this point, Karl Marx agreed with Durkheim: "Religion is only the illusory sun about which man revolves so long as he does not revolve about himself" (Marx [1843–1844] 1978: 54). "Illusory" is the key word here, for Marx was concerned that, although humans made their gods, they came to believe that their gods had made them. Where, to borrow a phrase from the anthropologist Edward Schieffelin, people "create the meaning[s] they discover" through religious ritual (Schieffelin 1985: 719), Marx worried that they failed to discover that they had, indeed, created these meanings. For Marx, the illusory symbols of religion masked "the *truth of this world*"—a singular reality that lay behind whatever mask people placed upon it (Marx [1843–1844] 1978: 54).

Philosophers working in the phenomenological tradition have taken issue, however, with Marx's conception of the relationship between reality and meaning. From the phenomenological perspective, reality exists only through its apperception. "Symbolic forms," Ernst Cassirer wrote, "are not imitations, but *organs* of reality, since it is solely by their agency that anything real becomes an object for intellectual apprehension" (1946: 8). From the phenomenologist's perspective, people do not merely make meaning; in the process of making meaning, they also make the worlds they imbue with it. As they do so through various and diverse languages and symbolic repertoires, phenomenologists have asserted, people create different—albeit potentially interpenetrating, or intersubjective—realities. In the words of the linguist Edward Sapir, upon whose work phenomenologists have drawn, "the 'real world' is to a large extent unconsciously built up on the language habits of the group. No two languages are ever sufficiently similar to be considered as representing the same social reality. The worlds in which different societies live are distinct worlds, not merely the same world with different labels attached" ([1929] 1949: 162).[2]

Building upon the phenomenological tradition, Greg Urban has asserted: "If truth is carried in discourse, and if discourse is completely embedded in the human populations in which it circulates, then to study the nature of truth and knowledge, we need to study the ways in which discourse—and hence truth— varies from one part of our globe to the next" (1996: xi). In recent years, anthropologists around the globe have taken a phenomenological approach to discursive formations reproduced within the rubric of occult cosmologies, including witchcraft, sorcery, shamanism, and spirit possession (e.g., Csordas 1994a, 1994b, 1997; Good 1994; Jackson 1989; Kapferer 1997; Stoller 1995).[3] Viewed in this way, "sorcery practices are more than a representation," according to Bruce Kapferer, "they are exercises in the construction and destruction of the psychosocial realities that human beings live and share. Their potency as representations results from this" (1997: 301–302); he has concluded, "sorcery highlights that truly extraordinary capacity of human beings to create and destroy the circumstances of their existence" (xi).[4] A phenomenological approach encourages us to ask what sort of world—or, to use the phenomenological term, "life-world" (*Lebenswelt*)—Muedans make and engage with through sorcery discourse. In other words, it prompts us to ask, not if Muedan sorcerers and the lions that they make (or that they become) are "real" or "illusory," but instead to what kind of reality they belong.

In seeking to answer this question, ironically, we discover that the life-world Muedans make through sorcery discourse comprises *two domains*: one visible, the other invisible.[5] According to those with whom we spoke, sorcerers used a medicinal substance called *shikupi* to render themselves invisible. Invisibility allowed them to escape the strictures and constraints of the visible world, to get "outside" or "beyond" the world experienced by ordinary Muedans. Having transcended the visible realm, sorcerers were able to see it without being seen and hence to act decisively upon it. Indeed, through their collective acts, sorcerers produced and sustained an invisible realm that afforded them powerful perspective on the world inhabited by their potential victims—a platform from which to mount their ghastly forays. Sorcerers thus remade the world in accordance with their destructive visions of a world transformed to their benefit.

Such "sorcerers of ruin" (*vavi va kwanongo*), as Muedans called them, were not alone in their use of *shikupi*—not alone in their ability to render themselves invisible. Beneficent authorities, including healers, settlement heads (in days of old), and village authorities (more recently), were said to challenge destructive sorcerers by themselves entering into the invisible realm, wherein they monitored, controlled, and even unmade sorcery of ruin by inverting, overturning, reversing, negating, or annulling it (all glossed by the Shimakonde verb *kupilikula*). To achieve this, they were required to further transcend the world known to ordinary Muedans—to "move beyond" the world of destructive sorcery and to practice "sorcery of construction" (*uwavi wa kudenga*). Such figures of authority were assumed by Muedans to be sorcerers themselves (for how else would they be able to enter the invisible realm of sorcery?), but they were assumed, or at least hoped, to be "cured," "reformed," or "retired" sorcerers who exercised their power to constructive ends.

Even as Muedans conceived of the visible and the invisible as distinct domains, then, they also understood these domains to be linked. As Muedans described the relationship between these domains, the invisible existed *within* the visible, and the visible *within* the invisible. The cosubstantiality of these domains was made manifest and apparent through the visible effects of invisible forces. Sorcerers, in other words, envisioned the world *and* brought their visions to fruition. Among other things, they imaginatively produced lions that ultimately came to prowl the same, visible, realm in which their victims lived, as Lazaro Mmala reminded me in the ARPAC seminar room. That Muedans thought of, and spoke of, sorcery lions differently than they did ordinary lions—*vantumi va ku mwitu* (bush lions)—bore evidence of their recognition that such beasts originated in a realm apart, a distinct domain. From the safety of distance in space or time, Muedans often referred to such lions as "false"—*vantumi kulambidyanga* (untruthful lions). Alternatively, they called them *vantumi va malao* (magical lions) or *vantumi va kumpika* (fabricated, or made up, lions). When, however, such beasts were encountered in or around the village—in other words, within the visible realm—Muedans fled them just the same.

Masked and Dangerous

We participate in this world through its illusions, and *as* its illusions. The inventions in which it is realized are only rendered possible through the phenomenon of control and the masking that accompanies it, and the conventional distinctions in which control is grounded can only be carried forth by being re-created in the course of invention.

« ROY WAGNER, *The Invention of Culture* (1975: 53–54) »

In August 1999, Marcos and I sat together around a small fire in the compound of his Matambalale relatives, warming ourselves after a meal of *ugwali* (cornmeal porridge) and roasted chicken. Out of the darkness emerged the figures of three of Marcos's kin. They had been youngsters when I first met them in 1994, but they had come of age now and served as core members of the village militia. Were we not "family" to them, I might have found them intimidating owing to their shared penchant for drunkenness and bluster. As it was, they often joined us, and other members of their family, after nightfall to exchange stories. It was from them that I first heard about the "sorcery dance."[1]

"The guys in this dance troupe all live in Shitashi," one of them told me. "They perform a dance that shows *exactly* how sorcerers eat human flesh."

The next morning, another young man appeared in the compound, sent by our young relatives to speak with us. He told us that he was in Matambalale visiting his own relatives, but that he was a member of the Shitashi dance troupe. Later in the day, he accompanied us in our pickup truck as we descended the plateau at Namakande and made our way to the steamy village of Shitashi in the lowlands near Lake Nguri. There, we were introduced to Fernando Chofer Nankoma, a young man of perhaps twenty-four or twenty-five years of age, *chefe* (leader) of the dance troupe. Chofer explained to us that he and his dancers performed for a fee of 50,000 meticais[2] at *matanga* (funeral) ceremonies.[3] He agreed to organize a performance for us for the same fee in a week's time.

When we returned on the appointed day, we found Chofer napping, but as the afternoon sun relented, his troupe of eight dancers appeared. Beneath two enormous mango trees, they constructed an enclosure in which the dance would be held. They then retreated to the edge of the village, where they dressed for the dance. As the sun set, younger boys set fires inside the enclosure and heated the skins of their drums in the flames. Near dusk, the dancers reappeared. One was dressed in a trench coat and wore a crown of porcupine quills. Another sported a pair of aviator glasses. Each dancer wore leg wraps to which dozens of ball-shaped bells had been attached. With every step, they jangled. Their leader was dressed as a *lipiko*—a figure, representing a spiritual entity, that historically appeared to dance at various Makonde ceremonies (including, especially, rites of initiation), striking fear into the hearts of all who remained ignorant of the *lipiko*'s "true" identity.[4] Not a patch of skin revealed the human figure within the *lipiko* costume. His torso, waist, and limbs were tightly wrapped in cloth. He wore a straw skirt around his midsection, a helmet mask over his head, and gloves on his hands.[5]

Out of the cacophony of noises produced by the young boys warming and testing the drum skins, there emerged, in time, a coordinated rhythm. The dancers entered the enclosure and moved in short stutter steps around its circumference. One of the drummers broke away from the fire and approached the dancers. Turning ninety degrees inward toward the drummer, leaning forward at the waist, hands in front of them, arms bent slightly, the dancers rose to the challenge of his distinctive beat until the drummer retired to the fire. The dancers then circled round the enclosure until the next drummer approached and challenged them. From time to time, observers—boys and girls, elder men and elder women—joined in, following the principal dancers' trail around the circle. For hours, they danced.[6]

By midnight, a crowd of several hundred had gathered in and around the enclosure. The drumming came to a halt, and Chofer announced that, in a short time, the troupe would stage a performance in the enclosure.[7] The principal dancers left, and a few colleagues prepared the "stage." A reed mat, curled into a semicircle, was stood on end, and a *capulana*[8] draped over it, making a tiny hut. A small pot was placed on the ground inside the hut.

Half an hour after they had disappeared, the dancers re-emerged from the darkness and drew close to the enclosure. Led by the *lipiko,* the others were naked except for white loincloths. Had it been darker, I was told, they would have been completely naked—"as sorcerers actually are." A lone dancer ran across the stage and back to the edge of the enclosure to concentrate the audience's attention. A few minutes later, another did the same. The audience at once grew more attentive and more impatient. Another dancer ran in front of them and said boldly, "Don't smoke any cigarettes! If you do, you'll be provoking those of us who have none!" With this public-service announcement made, the performance began.

The troupe stutter-stepped their way into the enclosure, led by the *lipiko.* I was now informed by a young companion of the dancers that this *lipiko* was the most sophisticated and lethal of all sorcerers.[9] On their second pass in front of the hut, the *lipiko* entered the dwelling and, there, discovered the small pot. The pot, I was told, was the flesh of the hut's owner, who—unseen to us but falling within the gaze of the sorcerer bearers of *shikupi*—slept unawares. The *lipiko* pulled several unseen portions of flesh from the pot and thrust them in his mouth. Several onlookers let loose expressions of horror: "Eeeeeee!"

Once the *lipiko* had departed the hut, a figure emerged from the edge of the stage carrying a bottle. He was an *nkulaula* (healer), I was told. He had been summoned by the owner of the house—who was now suffering from the *lipiko*'s attack—and the bottle he carried was a *lipande* (an antisorcery mine).

When the players passed once more in front of the house, they began, one by one, to convulse and, eventually, to fall to the ground in apparent agony. The onlookers laughed nervously. One among the players, whose face was painted in white, kept his feet and approached the *lipiko*—also left standing—who gave him a small gourd and an angled stick. With these instruments, he approached his writhing colleagues. After placing the gourd on the body of each one, he used the stick to turn them over onto their backs without touching them. It was explained to me that this painted sorcerer was the most experienced of the group; having been injured before, he had learned how to heal the wounds inflicted by antisorcery *mitela*. He slithered over the bodies of his fellow sorcerers, working on them as an *nkulaula*, administering the *mitela* provided him by the *lipiko*. As he turned their bodies, he "overturned" (*kupilikula*) the *nkulaula* who had been summoned to protect the victim of their attack and thereby rendered this victim vulnerable once more.[10]

The *lipiko* now gave the white-faced sorcerer-healer the pot, from which he doled out portions of human flesh to each of the colleagues he had resuscitated. One by one, the recipients placed the flesh in their mouths, alternately grimacing and licking their lips like snakes. The audience studied their every gesture, whispering commentary to one another. Some of the sorcerers displayed surprise, even revulsion, at the taste of the meat, which was bitter, I was told, as a result of the lingering effect of defensive *mitela*. Still, the sorcerers scuffled over their portions. The white-faced sorcerer himself consumed the greatest portions, but also ensured that each of his colleagues was fed, placing them, I was reminded, in his debt.

Once all had eaten, the white-faced sorcerer returned the pot to the hut, where the *lipiko* sat waiting. The *lipiko* now placed the pot on his head, rose, and danced his way out of the enclosure, followed by the other sorcerers. The owner of the house, I was told, was dead.

The performance over, Marcos and I spent the night in Shitashi. I scarcely slept. The images I had witnessed played again and again in my mind's eye. I lay awake in the darkness, attentive to every sound. The abundance of noise in the village around me gave testimony to the fact that I was not alone in my insomnia.

The next morning, Marcos and I shared a meal with Fernando Chofer Nankoma before departing Shitashi. I confessed that I had slept poorly. Chofer told us that the performance of their piece always produced sleepless nights, no matter where it was staged.

The same was true, Marcos said, of masquerade in the days of his youth. "Of course, when I was young, only initiated men knew that it was just a man behind the mask of the *lipiko* and not a spirit," Marcos explained.

"Nowadays, everyone knows who plays the *lipiko*," I commented; indeed, FRELIMO had considered *mapiko* dancing a means of propagating "obscurantism" and had required dancers to unmask themselves in front of their audiences from the time of the liberation war onward.

"They also know who plays the parts of the sorcerers in your drama," I continued, looking at Chofer, "but even so, they do not sleep at night?"

"Neither did the men who knew the identity of the *lipiko* back in the days before FRELIMO," Marcos chimed in.

Notwithstanding the unmasking of the dancers—Chofer and Marcos each asserted—spirits, and sorcerers, still existed for Muedans, who feared the very real consequences of encounter with them.[11]

Chofer continued: "We stage this piece to show people exactly what sorcery looks like. It is our way of criticizing sorcery. We perform to shame those who do these things."[12]

As I pondered Chofer's assertion that his troupe's performance somehow "re-presented" a "reality" "behind the mask"—that it conjured a world that existed, somewhere, separately, "offstage"—I suddenly remembered my conversation with an elder man standing beside me the night before as I watched Chofer's troupe perform.

"You see the way they eat human flesh?!" he asked me, genuinely scandalized.

"But surely they are just *acting out* what they *imagine* sorcerers do?" I responded.

"Exactly," the man replied, as if my words proved his point.

I looked at him with confusion.

"Who can imagine such a thing without doing it?!" he asked me, clinching his case.

What we witnessed, my fellow observer insisted, were sorcerers at work. What is more, he assured me, the message these "players" transmitted to their audience was precisely this: that they were *capable* sorcerers, to be respected and feared.[13]

I now pondered the idea that, even as Muedans imagined sorcery, they experienced these imaginings as real. Sorcery's reality lay neither in a mask that might be removed nor, somehow, behind a mask—neither "onstage" nor "offstage"—but rather was instantiated through its masking(s). In the moment of performative representation, the realities of the performance and the performed coexisted within one another.[14]

I turned to Chofer and asked him bluntly if my fellow observer had been correct in interpreting the performance we witnessed as sorcery.

"Perhaps," he answered.

I realized at once that I had backed Chofer into a corner and wondered if he was giving ground to avoid confrontation with me. "But you aren't sorcerers, are you?" I asked, rhetorically, hoping to alleviate the tension produced by my secondhand accusation.

To my surprise, Chofer looked at me pensively, though apparently unperturbed and unoffended. "I don't know," he answered, earnestly.[15]

Articulated Visions

Whereas all Muedans with whom we worked were susceptible to being accused of sorcery, few, if any, publicly claimed to be sorcerers.[1] Even as we made sorcery the explicit object of my ethnographic investigations, we encountered no one who openly asserted that he or she was a sorcerer. We nonetheless attended with great frequency conversations *about* the occurrence of sorcery. We participated in fireside chats where people made sense of illness or the death of a family member by reference to sorcery. We heard people accuse others of sorcery—sometimes in their presence, although generally not. We heard others deny accusations leveled against them. We heard second-, third-, and fourthhand rumors, and layer upon layer of innuendo.

Notwithstanding the ubiquity of witchcraft discourse (i.e., *talk about* witches and witchcraft) among Azande, Evans-Pritchard confidently asserted that "witches, as the Azande conceive them, clearly cannot exist" ([1937] 1976: 18).[2] Following this, I might attempt to distinguish between sorcery and sorcery discourse, concluding that the former did not exist and that the latter—despite its status as a corpus of accessible "social facts"—existed only as a set of, albeit logical, untruths. Sorcery lions, I might conclude, were made, not by sorcerers in an invisible realm, but instead by ordinary, self-deceived Muedans. As such, I might conclude, they were not flesh and blood and teeth and claws but rather mere verbal constructs, and ultimately false ones at that.

Jeanne Favret-Saada, who studied witchcraft in the Bocage region in rural western France, has suggested, however, that it is virtually impossible to disentangle witchcraft from the words through which people speak *of* it. One cannot speak sensibly *about* witchcraft, she has argued, without entering into the social relations and verbal exchanges that *constitute* witchcraft (1980: 10). The *reality* of witchcraft, she has asserted, *is discursive* (9). What Favret-Saada has argued in relation to witchcraft in the Bocage may also be said of sorcery in Mueda. Muedans, like me, engaged with the world of sorcery in a discursive field to which they themselves made substantial contributions. Not only did they, like me, experience sorcery's reality *through* its verbal constructs, but they conceived of sorcery and the words that spoke its reality as one and the same.

As already described, sorcerers were said to escape the constraints of the visible world by rendering themselves invisible and using the invisible realm thereby produced as a platform from which to elaborate self-serving visions of a world transformed. They were said not only to elaborate destructive visions of the world but also to *articulate* their visions on the canvas of Muedan society. Indeed, Muedans were adept at deciphering the traces of such articulations not only in the occurrence of illness and misfortune in their midst but also in discourse among themselves. Take, for example, the case of Sefu Assani Kuva (recounted in greater detail elsewhere [West 2005a: xiii–xxviii]). Sefu was accused of fabricating lions and using them to attack his neighbors in the village of Kilimani. As evidence in support of their accusations against him, Kilimani residents told the post administrator presiding over his trial that he had once brazenly boasted: "Don't mess with me! If I want to, I can make a lion and kill you!"[3] These words—whose origins and peregrinations proved impossible to document—simultaneously constituted the threat, the accusation, the evidence, and the enactment of

[margin note: sorcery + reality through verbal]

sorcery. Framed in and stripped of quotations marks several times over, they not only spoke *of* sorcery but also *spoke* sorcery. Without them, Sefu's lions were, quite literally, unimaginable— to him, to his neighbors, to the post administrator, and to the anthropologist. With them—indeed, *within* them—Sefu's lions came to life.

[handwritten margin note: enact sorcery with threat]

If Muedan sorcerers discursively unmade the world in accordance with their predatory visions, countersorcerers discursively remade it in accordance with their reconstructive visions. To do so, they not only elaborated transcendent visions of a world remade but also *articulated* these within Muedan society. The force of countersorcerers, in fact, depended upon the persuasiveness of their metadiscursive commentaries on prior elements of sorcery discourse. Through their various methods, healers worked to convince their patients that *their* perspectives surpassed those of the attackers whose lethal visions they undid. Healers openly demeaned those with whom they did battle, saying to their patients things like "This illness that afflicts you is only *made up*." Healers dealing with sorcery lions similarly highlighted these beasts' inventedness: "This thing is just a *made* thing." By affirming to their patients that their afflictions—indeed, their realities—were discursively produced, healers rendered these afflicted realities susceptible to *metadiscursive* transformation.[4] Similarly, settlement heads of old—and village authorities more recently—moved through their settlements in the wee hours of the morning, patrolling sorcery in their domains by painting verbal pictures of the invisible realm: "I see you!" they would proclaim in loud, authoritative voices, heard by settlement residents lying in their beds. "I know who you are—you *vavi* who are killing people in my settlement!" They gained ascendancy over chaos in their world by modeling order for all to hear—by orally conceiving *of*, and thus *conceiving*, a new world. Their *words* constituted the *enactment* of their "sorcery of construction." By declaring that they knew what sorcerers "were up to," these beneficent authorities disarmed them. Their power to do so lay in the persuasive force of their articulated visions.

[handwritten margin note: orally conceiving a new world]

Even ordinary Muedans remade their world through their contributions to sorcery discourse. In the colonial period, for example, sorcery accusations circulated wildly around the material goods that labor migrants brought home with them from Tanganyika. Returnees generally considered envious villagers as potential sorcerers who might seek to destroy what they had made *for* themselves and *of* themselves.[5] Villagers, for their part, looked upon returnees with suspicion, asking how these young men (and, occasionally, young women) had been able to accrue such wealth if not by feeding off others, a predilection they feared would persist back home. Each side accused the other of sorcery.[6] Ironically, where labor migrants suspected and feared the leveling force of sorcery practiced against them, their *accusations* constituted a discursive force in defense of their accumulation of unprecedented riches, rendering would-be levelers suspect.[7] At the same time, where villagers expressed suspicions of illegitimate accumulation on the part of returning labor migrants, their accusations served to quash rampant forms of social differentiation.[8] Either way, sorcery discourse constituted a tangible force in the world, inverting (*kupilikula*) the invisible force it simultaneously attested to.[9]

Such dynamics were in play during the period in which I conducted fieldwork as well. When an agricultural credit scheme allowed Muedans of means to acquire tractors, trucks, and grain mills below market cost, rumors spread about how the new owners of these objects—mostly ranking government and party officials—had been able to acquire such prized possessions and defend them from envious onlookers. It was often suggested that these "big chiefs" had gained and sustained these goods in league with fellow sorcerers, to whom they had sacrificed members of their own families—often children.[10] It was also said that their machines were defended by *lindandosho*, the zombie slaves of sorcerer deed-holders.[11] Through sorcery discourse, ordinary Muedans thus critiqued sorcery as an accumulative force for personal gain and, in so doing, placed acute pressure on the owners of these goods to share the wealth they generated.[12] Owners, of course, saw the situation from a decidedly different perspective. Within a short time, their trucks, tractors, and grain mills began to break down. Owners suspected that their machines were falling prey to sorcerers in the villages through which they passed or in which they were installed. With their machines out of service and repair bills piling up and eating into the profits that owners had hoped to make, owners reported being told by the healers they consulted that sorcerers had paralyzed these machines by stuffing human skulls and other body parts inside them. Through their own contributions to sorcery discourse, then, these elites defended their rights to individual accumulation and economic differentiation, turning a critical eye on those who would, by their leveling attacks, destroy anything and everything of value.[13]

Whether wealthy or poor, powerful or weak, Muedans not only accused others of perpetrating sorcery against them but simultaneously transcended those they accused by fixing them in their gaze, declaring knowledge of "what they were up to" and, thereby, undoing them (*kupilikula*). In some cases, the undoing of accused sorcerers took lethal form; in the wake of lion attacks that claimed forty-six lives and left another six people seriously injured in late 2002 and early 2003, for example, eighteen residents of Muidumbe District were accused of sorcery and lynched.[14] Sorcery and countersorcery were cosubstantial in these discursive acts of endless one-upmanship—acts that animated the very real unmaking and remaking of the Muedan world and those who inhabited it.

Greg Urban has written: "Discourse is about the world (it is the bearer of truth, statements, meanings), but discourse is also in the world. It has a thing-like quality, and it is that quality that makes circulation (and hence culture) possible" (1996: xiii). Along similar lines, Raymond Williams has argued that "language and signification [are] indissoluble elements of the material social process itself" (1977: 99). Not only does Muedan sorcery discourse confirm this, but Muedans themselves sometimes explicitly reflected upon it. Muedans with whom we worked said that those who "knew a little something" *about* sorcery—like healers and settlement heads—in fact *knew* sorcery; those who *articulated* visions of sorcery's workings *were* sorcerers; *talk* about sorcery *was* sorcery; words and deeds were cosubstantial.

Little wonder my fellow observer considered the dancer Chofer and his troupe to be sorcerers, for they boldly displayed their vision of the invisible realm for all to see. While theirs was a *commentary on* sorcery—purportedly offered as a *restraining critique of* sorcery—their articulated vision bore evidence of their capabilities *as sorcerers.* Like all "sorcerers of construction," they were the objects of popular ambivalence—of speculation as to whether they used their power to socially beneficial, or socially destructive, ends.

While no Muedan—not even healers, not even settlement heads or village authorities, not to mention Chofer—claimed to be a sorcerer, the broadly held notion that articulated visions of sorcery *constituted* sorcery left most to wonder not only about others but, occasionally, about themselves, as Chofer did when I asked him if he was a sorcerer. After all, every Muedan spoke—if only in hushed tones—*about* sorcery. Everyone, at some moment, articulated a vision of the invisible world, no matter how sketchy. Everyone contributed to sorcery discourse. If discursive and metadiscursive engagements with reality constituted means of (re)producing reality, if sorcerers of ruin and sorcerers of construction (re)made the world by articulating visions of the world remade, if even gossip and innuendo afforded means by which ordinary people inverted the invisible forces to which they alluded, in short, if every constitutive vision of the world *was sorcery,* was the healer Atanásio Herneo not right: was not everyone a sorcerer?

everyone contributes to sorcery discourse

Bridging Domains

That the Muedan life-world comprised two domains—one invisible, in which sorcery lions were made; the other visible, in which these beasts wreaked havoc—gives us cause to return to the question of lions as metaphors. Metaphor derives from the Greek *metaphora*, meaning "to transfer" or "to carry across" (*meta*, "trans"; *pherein*, "to carry") (Soskice 1985: 1). Sorcerers, according to Muedans with whom we worked, not only made lions under the cloak of invisibility but also transported these lions from the invisible realm to the visible, where they attacked their victims. This act of transference warrants close attention.

Sister Rosa Carla did not dispute Muedans' claims that the lion she carried in the back of her pickup truck was "real." Nor do I think she objected to Muedans "telling stories"—morality tales—with "imaginary" lions as protagonists; during the year I conducted dissertation research in Mueda, the Walt Disney Corporation released the film *The Lion King*, a production which I imagine Sister Rosa Carla might have recognized and accepted as such a tale. What she and others with whom I spoke could not countenance, however, was the notion that people could "make up" "real" lions. They objected to the idea that lions born of an imaginary, invisible domain came to occupy the visible domain of ordinary people—that they moved between these domains, attacking the rivals and enemies of their makers, producing macabre effects. Yet this is precisely what Muedans asserted sorcery lions did.[1]

It might be argued here that Muedans confused semantic and ontological domains: that the invisible domain, and the sorcery lions produced therein, were merely ideas, while the visible domain, along with ordinary lions (bush lions), properly existed. Such transference of lions from one domain to the other might be dismissed as an errant Muedan superimposition of semantic sorcery lions onto ontological bush lions.[2] Following Cassirer (1946), however, we might instead conclude that Muedans conceived *of,* and thus *conceived,* a world of two domains: that both the visible domain and the invisible were, at once, *imagined and real;* that through their perception of the world, Muedans *made* each of these domains, and the constitutive relations between them.[3]

Dorothy Lee has argued: "Symbols are a part of the process whereby the experienced world, the world of perception and concept, is created out of the world of physical reality" (1959: 79). As such, symbols do not refer to a separate world but instead constitute an essential part of the world of which they speak. Along these lines, Roy Wagner has argued that "neither signifier nor signified belongs to the established order of things," that symbolization constitutes "the act of invention in which form and inspiration come to figure each other," and that "[t]hus the tension and contrast between symbol and symbolized collapse[s], and we may speak of such a construction as a 'symbol' that stands for itself" (1975: 43).[4] Symbols, in other words, articulate the relationships that they create with, and within, the world that is conceived through them.[5]

Whereas James Siegel has suggested that the "'truth' of magic is the power inherent in language to conjoin" and that shamans, in the cases with which he is concerned, achieve this conjunction by "say[ing], in effect, that 'this' . . . is 'that'" (2003: 148, 149), Muedans with whom we worked effectively said that what is imagined is real—that the sorcerer is a lion. In discursively producing sorcery lions, and in moving them from one domain to another, Muedans in fact accomplished what James Fernandez has called one of "the mission(s) of metaphor" (1974). With sorcery lions, Muedans in fact bridged the chasm between distinct domains upon which metaphor depends for its force.[6] In so doing, they brought about a transference not only in semantic space but also in physical-perceptual space. Stefano Cochetti has labeled such "material substitutions" (a category that he has suggested includes sacrifice as well) "literal metaphors" (1995: 144–145, 150). Such metaphors not only stand for themselves, I would argue, but also *embody* themselves—in the Muedan case, in the bodies of dangerous predators.[7]

George Lakoff and Mark Johnson have argued: "In all aspects of life . . . we define our reality in terms of metaphors and then proceed to act on the basis of the metaphors. We draw inferences, set goals, make commitments, and execute plans, all on the basis of how we in part structure our experience, consciously and unconsciously, by means of metaphor" (1980: 158). By way of example, they have demonstrated how the metaphor "argument is war" in fact shapes the way we argue (4). Carol Laderman has similarly argued that metaphor "does not merely refer to or talk about but *does something* in the world" (1991: 3).[8] James Fernandez has reminded us that "[m]etaphors are not only rhetorical devices of persuasion; they can also lead to performance" (1974: 125). Consequently, the imaginative predication of a lion upon someone—whether George or Imbwambwe—does not leave him unaltered. Where Muedan sorcery discourse forged a metaphoric relationship between Imbwambwe and the lion he became, Muedans saw and interacted with Imbwambwe as never before.[9] Through such imaginative flights of reference, Muedans formed and transformed their understandings and experiences of the domains that they inhabited and the Imbwambwes with whom they shared them, changing their world fundamentally and irrevocably.

Lakoff and Johnson (1980) have argued that, because no world exists independently of our conception of it through lan-

we speak of word through metaphor

guage, we inevitably speak of the world *only* through metaphor. Wagner (1986) has described culture itself as layer upon layer of metaphor, with nothing else beneath it. If all discursive engagements with the world are inescapably metaphorical, perhaps the most interesting question is not, then, whether Muedan sorcerers' imaginings (among them, sorcery lions) are metaphors but rather whether metaphors (for that matter, all forms of discourse through which we conceive our worlds) constitute means of sorcery.

"A language, and, insofar as it can be said to have conventions (which is how we, perforce, describe it), a culture, is the ultimate subjunctive, an 'as if' made into an 'is' by the *seriousness* of those who use it" (Wagner 1986: 8, emphasis added).[10] Perhaps the only difference between the speaker of the phrase "George is a lion" and the sorcerer-producer of an *ntumi wa kumpika* lies in their degree of *seriousness* of imagination. Some people, Muedans realized, are dangerously serious.

Working with Indeterminacy

If sorcery discourse constituted literal, or embodied, metaphors by which Muedans perceived and engaged with their world, sorcery was not the only language through which their world was conceived. In 1994, and again in 1999, nationwide multiparty elections were held in Mozambique to elect the president of the republic and members of Parliament. Through the electoral process, Muedans were introduced to the discourse of liberal democracy—a discourse whose animating logics differed greatly from those of sorcery. In the run-up to the vote, elections organizers (Mozambicans supported materially and logistically by numerous donor nations and a plethora of international organizations) articulated their own vision for the rationalization of power and the profound transformation of politics in postwar Mozambique. In accordance with their vision, elections organizers instructed Mozambicans to register to vote by having their photos taken and voter identification cards issued to them. These cards, and the bureaucratic electoral apparatus to which they were attached, may be said to have operated as a vast material metaphor (West 2003).

Elections organizers concerned with ensuring the credibility of electoral results—both to observers and to participants—suggested that the electoral apparatus effectively rendered the nation visible to itself in the moment of expression of the national political will. Within the electoral bureaucracy, each voter card and, later, each ballot paper operated as a metonymic extension of an individual Mozambican. The political will of that voter was made manifest by an X marked on his or her ballot card, which could be folded to conceal from observers the choice that he or she had made. When later removed from the ballot box and unfolded, each card represented for all to see the will of a single anonymous voter. Just as voter cards and ballots were standardized, the weight—the value—of each voter's will was equal. Ultimately, the political legitimacy of each winning candidate was made manifest in the relative height and weight of the stack of ballot cards with Xs marked beside his or her name and photographic image compared with the height and weight of other stacks of ballot cards with Xs marked beside other candidates' names and images. In this way, the elections process—as "literal metaphor"—was said both to *represent* and, simultaneously, to *enact* the confidential, yet transparent, measurement of the will of the Mozambican people and, hence, to rationalize political forces that heretofore had exercised power in hidden, arbitrary, and irrational ways.

Whether or not elections officials explicitly conceived of the electoral apparatus as metaphor, they vested faith in the notion that this apparatus afforded to Mozambicans a means of simplifying and clarifying an inchoate world, as Fernandez has told us metaphors do (1972: 43–44). Officials acted *as if* power could *actually* be rendered *transparent* and, thereby, rationalized so long as conditions were created for monitoring the electoral process *as through a pane of glass.*

To the astonishment and frustration of elections officials, however, many Muedans refused to register for the vote in 1994 (West 1997, 2003). Elder Muedans, in particular, associated voter cards with other identity tokens with which they had had experience in their lifetimes, including colonial tax receipts, mandatory labor cards and passbooks, church-issued Virgin Mary medallions, and FRELIMO party membership cards

(West 2003). Each of these identity tokens had been used by powerful institutions to mark Muedans, making possible various historical forms of surveillance through which they were monitored, controlled, and often brutally exploited. Elders were loath to allow themselves to be marked once more by political actors whom they suspected of wishing to further manipulate them.

In spurning the notion that they, as voters, might control these actors, Muedan elders did not "fail to understand the electoral process" (as more than one elections official hypothesized in conversation with me). Nor did they sequester themselves within a limited, local worldview, as others opined. Rather, they understood the electoral process differently, experiencing it through the sensory organs of sorcery discourse. Indeed, they fixed elections officials within a scrutinizing gaze that transcended these officials' limited views of the Muedan world.

As elections officials moved about the plateau region in United Nations vehicles and aircraft, Muedans watched with suspicion. Several shared accounts with me in which they portrayed these vehicles as the instruments of sorcery attack. "Crash sites" had been found, I was told, devoid of visible remains but marked by mysterious circles of flattened bush—evidence of night flights by "untruthful," "fabricated" aircraft. In a world filled with such brazen new powers—undoubtedly in league with local agents of sorcery—many Muedans doubted that their votes would remain "secret." Surely, the powers vying for their votes and proclaiming their intentions to remake Mozambique were all capable sorcerers and, thus, all able to see invisible ballots and hold those who cast them accountable (see also Hanlon 1995: 42; Synge 1997: 129).

In reading the "transition to democracy" through sorcery discourse, Muedans (re)constructed the world that elections officials worked to build.[1] Ironically, where the discourse of liberal democracy explicitly empowered Muedans to (re)make their world, sorcery discourse provided means through which Muedans reflected upon, and often accentuated, limitations to their abilities to make the world as elections officials suggested they

might do. Through the accusations, denials, rumors, and in-
nuendos that constituted sorcery discourse, Muedans had long
reminded themselves of their limited abilities to (re)make their
world. While, through sorcery discourse, Muedans expressed
suspicions that some among them were capable of incredible
things, they generally conceived of themselves as the objects
upon which sorcery was enacted—as passive victims, rather
than active perpetrators, of definitive power. Even the sorcerers among them possessed limited capacities to (re)make their
world, most Muedans averred. The transformative power of sorcery, as Muedans conceived it, proved unwieldy in the pursuit of
strategic ends—resistant to instrumentalization.[2] Sorcery, as the
healer Sinema Kakoli described it to us, was a game of Russian
roulette: as healers provided most potential victims of sorcery
attack with sorcery prophylaxis, and laid *mapande* (countersorcery mines) in and around nearly everything that sorcerers might wish to destroy, it was only a matter of time before
sorcerers mortally wounded themselves. Kakoli thus expressed
awareness of what Webb Keane has referred to as the "hazards
of representation"—the possibility that the act of signification,
in which great power potentially rests, may indeed "go wrong"
(1997: 25). As powerful as sorcerers were, Kakoli told me, "they
waste no time dying."

Countersorcerers, and even ordinary Muedans, similarly
found sorcery discourse an unwieldy and perilous instrument.
In time, authority figures and healers inevitably suffered the
consequences of speaking ill of one more powerful than they.[3]
Even those who engaged the invisible realm through rumor, innuendo, suspicion, and accusation did so with great risk (often
with disastrous effect) and only because they knew that ignorance of sorcery was as perilous an option as any.[4] Ultimately,
all Muedans—whether powerful or weak, envied or envious,
knowledgeable or ignorant—were undone by sorcery.

"Men make their own history," Marx wrote, "but they do not
make it just as they please; they do not make it under circumstances chosen by themselves, but under circumstances directly

found, given and transmitted from the past" ([1852] 1978: 595). As Muedans (re)made their world through sorcery discourse, they spoke a language—and made use of a symbolic repertoire—not entirely of their own invention. The sense of this polyvalent production often lay beyond the grasp of individual speaker/producers.[5] Thus, sorcery was not only a means by which Muedans made their world but also a means by which the world they encountered made them.[6]

Even so, sorcery constituted a discursive space in which Muedans could speak about the world and act within it in ways they could not through other discursive formations.[7] For most, the discourse of liberal democracy, for example, *oversimplified* an *inescapably inchoate* world. By contrast, sorcery discourse accentuated the ambiguity of ongoing events and processes in the inchoate world of postsocialist Mozambique. If sorcery discourse served Muedans as metaphor, it more closely resembled metaphor as conceived of by Ann Game and Andrew Metcalfe—metaphor that "works with indeterminacy to keep meaning safe from the final clarification that is its obituary" (1996: 50).[8]

By expressing continuing suspicions of power in the democratic era through sorcery discourse, Muedans partially realized the world on their own terms and partially realized enduring constraints upon their abilities to do so. Indeed, sorcery discourse served Muedans well in their struggles to survive "on the margins" (as they were fond of saying) of the modern world. The "hidden transcript" (Scott 1990) sustained by Muedans through sorcery discourse told them that the operation of *power itself* remained hidden, notwithstanding the inception of liberal democracy.[9] Through reflection in and on the invisible domain of sorcery, Muedans sustained their understanding that the forces that animated social life were not always comprehensible, or readily manipulable. Sorcery discourse nurtured Muedan ambivalence toward power, reminding them both that power was essential to the creation of prosperity and social well-being and that truly decisive power generally operated in a realm accessible only to an extraordinary few.[10] Sorcery discourse facilitated

Muedan appreciation for the complex dilemmas created by the elusiveness and capriciousness of power in their midst. Those who did not enter with vigor into the fray remained vulnerable to being devoured, sorcery discourse reminded them, while those who played the games of power were destined, eventually, to lose. Sorcery discourse reminded Muedans that politics is an unavoidable and unending contest in which no victory is final, no defeat complete—a contest requiring constant surveillance and judgment of the contestants by participants and observers alike.[11]

Through sorcery discourse, Muedans reflected upon the complex truth that the world they made sometimes eluded their grasp, sometimes turned around and made them, and sometimes became suddenly and unexpectedly responsive to their whims.[12] Through the production of sorcery discourse, they reconciled themselves to the indomitable dialectics of social life. They resigned themselves to the idea that one cannot always truly see or know with certainty the reality in which one is suspended[13]— that one is sometimes left to trade secondhand accounts about how the world works, and why. Within sorcery discourse, Muedans perceived the irreducible complexity of their world even as they carried on making their world complex.

Doctors Kalamatatu

Despite frequent visits to Kalamatatu's home in the village of Matambalale—where I based myself most often and for the longest stints during fieldwork in 1994 and 1999—Marcos and I were never able to find his home without guidance from a village youth, even though it was clearly marked by one of the largest and most distinctive mango trees in the village. We joked often about this, wondering aloud if this powerful healer had ringed his home with camouflaging medicinal substances, as we were told healers sometimes did.

When I returned to Matambalale in 1999, we were able for the first time to locate Kalamatatu's yard unaided. The elder had died. As we stood wistfully, taking in the scene of the healer's abandoned compound, I realized that I had no picture of the yard, his and his wife's houses, and the tree. I had pulled my camera from my field bag and focused for a shot when I heard the voice of a woman, admonishing me.

"Why would you want a picture of that?!" she scolded me. "Of all the houses in this village, why must you take a picture of that one, in ruins? Why not take a picture of a house in good condition? We are proud too, you know!"

"No, Mama," Marcos called back to her, respectfully. "It's not because the house is in ruins that he's taking a picture."

The woman now stood only a few feet away. She remained perturbed.

Marcos put his hand on my back, looking at the woman. "This one," he said, "was a friend of the elder." He now pointed to the house. "Many times, he visited the old man in that house. He is taking a picture now as a remembrance of his friend."

The woman looked carefully at me. "Andiliki?" she said. "Is this Andiliki?"

I did not recognize her face. I did not know if she knew me by appearance or only by name. "I am Andiliki," I confessed.

She reached for my hand and greeted me. "You've come back to visit us!" she announced.

"Yes," I said.

Marcos then asked her if anyone in the village tended to Kalamatatu's affairs. She told us that we should speak to his nephew, who was away from the village but expected back in a few days.

When we returned on the appointed day, Marcos, Tissa, and I were met on the edge of Kalamatatu's yard by his son, Lipapa Kalamatatu. Lipapa took us to his own house, just a few dozen meters away. There, we sat in awkward but brief silence as we awaited the arrival of others whom Lipapa had summoned to join us. Within a short time, we were introduced to four other men: another son, Laja; a nephew (sister's son), Duarte Felipe; another nephew, Henrique Maulide; and a "younger *likola* brother" (probably a mother's sister's son), Calisto Simoni.

When all were assembled, Lipapa began to speak. Since we had last seen Kalamatatu, he told us, the elder had suffered from headaches and backaches. He became quite ill once, but recovered. Some time later, however, he fell ill again. This time, he did not recover. He died in 1996, Lipapa reported.

"Was this illness provoked by *uwavi* [sorcery]?" I asked.

"No," Lipapa responded, nonplussed. "It was a natural illness." His words were steady and assured. "It had nothing to do with *uwavi*. He wasn't attacked, nor did he injure himself."

I expressed my sentiments. "Kalamatatu was a good friend to me," I said, wondering if my words would be considered appropriate.

"*Namene* [very]," the entire group responded in unison with an enthusiasm that surprised me.

To this, Lipapa added: "It's true. You were great friends. The old man received your visits many times. He had great confidence in you."

I was not certain what Lipapa meant by "great confidence," but his statement filled me with a vague satisfaction.

Calisto Simoni told me that the photos I had given Kalamatatu were now kept in his house.

"When the elder died," Lipapa then said, "he left his *mitela* with three of us." Lipapa reached out and pinched the cloth of Calisto's and Henrique's tattered shirts, indicating the threesome who had inherited Kalamatatu's stores of medicinal substances. "Calisto holds the *mitela* in his house. But we work together."

Later, we sat with the three men and talked about their work as healers. The triumvirate they formed replicated one that had once included Kalamatatu, his *njomba* (mother's brother)/mentor, Mikuku, and Mikuku's younger brother. Collaboration not only made the responsibility of healing less onerous for each healer but also ensured the continuity of the *mitela* with which they worked. "Kalamatatu knew that he could die at any time," Lipapa told us. "He wanted to be sure that his *mitela* would survive, even if the one he passed it to died suddenly, unexpectedly."

Before conversing further with Kalamatatu's three successors, I requested that we visit Kalamatatu's grave so that I might pay my respects. My request was anticipated—perhaps even expected—and off we went, despite a surprise shower in the midst of this, the dry season.

A bulging mound of earth with a small wooden cross at one end marked Kalamatatu's resting place. Burned onto the cross with a hot iron were the letters "P A U L O." In his final moments, I learned, Kalamatatu had been baptized.

I gathered my thoughts for, now, I knew, I was expected to speak. I removed my hat, as did the others. I cleared my throat.

"Kalamatatu Ndudu Nankanda," I said, clearly, intentionally, as if my words might somehow overwrite the name on the wooden cross. "From the very first time I spoke with the *nang'olo* (elder), I knew that I could learn many things from him. He was a man of important wisdom. But it was the second time I met him that I remember most dearly. I introduced him by name, 'Kalamatatu,' to my colleague here." I looked at Marcos. "When he heard me pronounce his name correctly, he was so pleased that he told me, 'From now on, you, too, are Kalamatatu!'" Everyone laughed, gently. "He not only shared his knowledge with me, he shared his name." I reached into my pocket, where I had earlier placed one of my business cards. "When I visited him years ago, I gave him a card like this one with my name printed on it. He kept it, I know, because each time I returned, he retrieved it from his house and held it as we spoke." Again, we shared gentle laughter. "Well, now I have a new card for Kalamatatu. As I promised him, I have become a 'doctor.'"

"Doctor Andiliki." Marcos interjected with a smile.

"I could not have accomplished this without my friend, my teacher, Kalamatatu. He taught me what I had to know." Now looking at his three successors, I added, "and he was there with me when I was tested."

Indeed, he had been. On the day of my dissertation defense, I wore tied around my arm beneath my shirt the *ilishi* (small packet of *mitela*) that Kalamatatu had given me to ensure that I speak with the voice of a lion and that my words be respected.[1]

The elder's three successors nodded knowingly at my euphemism.

I felt a jag in my voice as I continued: "So now, as Kalamatatu shared his name with me, I share my title with him. We are doctors, he and I—Doctors Kalamatatu."

An affirming murmur surrounded me as I placed the card at the base of the wooden cross.

As I stepped back, Marcos initiated a Catholic prayer in Shimakonde. The others followed along as best they could. Where words sometimes failed them, the gesture of the cross did not.

We reconvened at Lipapa's house, where we spoke at length about their work, and about mine. I took their pictures, promising to give them copies when I next saw them. I then showed them pictures of my family. Among them were pictures of me, my partner, and my parents assembled around the larger-than-life stone sculpture of the Nittany Lion that sits on the campus of the Pennsylvania State University where my father taught. I explained that there were lions in Pennsylvania too, but that they were much smaller than the statue—and much smaller than the lions found in Mueda. Lipapa joked with me, saying that the photo was evidence that my family and I knew how to make lions of which we had no fear.

As we departed, Kalamatatu's successors assured me that his work was being carried on, and they asked that my friendship with him also be continued through them. Lipapa looked at me and cleared his throat. "As you were such a good friend of the elder," he said, "perhaps you can help us resolve one of our concerns." Where such a preamble might ordinarily have made me wary of the request to come, I found myself receptive—even eager to accommodate. "The elder is buried here in any old way. The rain beats down on his grave and, in time, it will disappear. We would like to preserve this site properly, but we need a sack of cement." Lipapa and his relatives wished to cover the grave with a slab of concrete, as they had seen done in cemeteries elsewhere, in Pemba, in Mocímboa da Praia, or in Tanzania.

I asked Marcos if cement could be purchased in any of the shops in the town of Mueda, and he assured me that it could. I asked if one of them could accompany us the next day when we departed for the town of Mueda, and Henrique was chosen. I would arrange the cement, I promised, as well as transport for Henrique to carry it back to Matambalale.

Lipapa clasped my hand. Before he let go, he offered words that he seemed to be holding on to until the moment of our parting. "Kalamatatu trusted you because he recognized in you a certain characteristic—a certain ability," he told me, looking me in the eyes. His facial expression was intense. His words remained unclear to me. I noticed, however, that Tissa looked at him with astonishment. "This is what allowed you to write your book," Lipapa added. "This is what allowed you to become a doctor."

Later, Tissa would explain to me that Lipapa's words euphemistically indicated that his father, Kalamatatu, thought of me as a sorcerer—a *fellow* sorcerer. "That certain characteristic," Tissa said, "that certain ability . . . it's *uwavi*! And the elder recognized it in you, his son was saying, because he knew it himself!"

Neither Lipapa nor Tissa specified what *kind* of sorcery Kalamatatu understood the two of us to practice.

Ethnographic Sorcery

"Well, now that we *have* seen each other," said the unicorn, "if you believe in me, I'll believe in you."
«LEWIS CARROLL, *Through the Looking-Glass* ([1871] 1998: 201)»

On the day that Mandia treated me, one of his three wives gave me reason to believe that he, too, considered me a colleague of sorts. Upon completion of my treatment, the *humu* rose to his feet and disappeared from the house in which we were seated. I later discovered that he was fetching a drum to be played while he danced in a ceremonial manner reserved to *vahamu* such as he. As we sat awaiting his return, however, his wife drew close to me and asked me, almost conspiratorially, what cures *I* knew. They were most concerned, she admitted, to learn if I knew how to cure chickens, for theirs, like everyone's in the village, were dying of a strange disease that neither the *humu* nor anyone else knew how to treat. The ailment she described to me reminded me of what I had heard of Newcastle disease. I told her that I thought chickens could be vaccinated against such diseases but, to her great disappointment, I informed her that I was no veterinarian.

The *humu* and his wives—as well as other Muedans with whom I worked—knew, however, that I did possess some medical knowledge. They might have learned this from Marcos, who frequently told the story of my having "saved" his infant son, Godinho. Indeed, in the first weeks that I worked with Marcos, the boy had fallen ill and, after several days without improvement, I looked in on him to discover him with a high fever, a stiff neck, and a swollen fontanel. I shared my suspicions of cerebral malaria with Marcos and insisted that the child be taken to the hospital, where my diagnosis was confirmed; we then postponed our first research trip to the plateau so that Marcos and I could monitor the quinine doses Godinho received from a less-than-dependable hospital staff.

My "healing knowledge" derived from three years' experience, while in college, working for tuition money as an attendant at the University of Virginia hospital, and three more years, during graduate school, on an ambulance crew in Madison, Wisconsin. I carried with me, in Mueda, an Emergency Medical Technician's jump kit and a copy of *Where There Is No Doctor* (Werner, Thuman, and Maxwell 1992), and I treated those who came to me so long as I was competent to do so.

In fact, the occasion eventually arose for me to treat Humu Mandia himself. Throughout my 1999 research stint on the Mueda plateau, I had regularly inquired as to the *humu*'s whereabouts with the young man he had appointed as his successor. He was in the lowlands, I was told, tending to his fields. Near the end of my time in Mueda, however, the young *humu* informed me that the elder had suffered an accident, tripping and falling into the cooking fire and badly burning himself. I wondered, out loud, if a *humu*—a man of great healing knowledge—could be taken to the hospital. "We intended to take him," the young *humu* told us, "but he was in such pain that we could not move him." I asked if it would be possible to fetch him with our pickup truck, but the young *humu* told us that there were no passable roads. In any case, he told us, he feared the elder would not survive the trip. As I was scheduled to fly out of Pemba in only a few days, there was no time for me to make the journey on foot to the elder's lowland fields. I was hesitant to suggest that I might somehow be able to assist this powerful healer with his own health, but I felt deeply indebted to him for having treated me when I had been ill. I wondered if he had taken me as his patient despite similar ambivalence. In any case, the young *humu* facilitated my decision on the matter by asking, "Is there anything that you can do for him? Do you have any medicines that will help?" I asked the young *humu* to describe the elder's burns as thoroughly as he could. From his description, the elder had suffered mostly first- and second-degree burns on a substantial portion of his back and shoulders, as well as second- and third-degree burns on the back sides of one leg and one arm. I provided the young *humu* with a large bottle of Betadine to disinfect the wounds. I also gave him a box of occlusive dressings and gauze wrap. I instructed him to cover the first- and second-degree burns and to build dressing tents over the more serious wounds. I described the effects of potential infection and gave him a course of antibiotics to administer should these appear, warning him to strictly follow dosage instructions and to cease administering the pills in case of allergic reaction. When I returned to Cabo Delgado in 2001, I was delighted to learn that the elder had recovered.

As a result of such incidents, many of those with whom I worked in Mueda considered me a healer of sorts.[1] Kalamatatu's comment, as expressed through his successor, about recognizing in me "a certain characteristic—a certain ability," went deeper than this, however. Kalamatatu, I later came to think, saw in me a young man eager to "know a little something" about how the world worked and how its ills might be cured. In my quest to understand sorcery, I spent hours a day, for months on end, with healers like Kalamatatu—as Lipapa, Henrique, and Calisto had done with Kalamatatu, and as Kalamatatu had done with Mikuku. As anthropological participant observer, I not only made myself a student of sorcery but sought to see (as Muedan healers and responsible authority figures did) beneath the surface of Muedan life, into the realm of hidden, but decisive, forces. The more conversant I became in the language of sorcery, the more often I heard Muedans say of me, *"Adju, andimanya shinu shoeshoe!"* (That one knows a little something!), a euphemism applied to sorcerers and countersorcerers alike.[2]

Ironically, notwithstanding Favret-Saada's assertion (1980) that witchcraft can be engaged only from within its constitutive dialogical spaces, in my attempts to discover the interior of the Muedan life-world of sorcery, I shared with Muedans the urge to somehow get outside that world, to move beyond it in order to gain perspective on it,[3] to formulate a transcendent vision of it. I eventually came to understand that Kalamatatu and other Muedans must have recognized the uneasy space of partial knowledge in which I consequently found myself—an anthropologically cliché space outside the comforts of ordinary life in both physical and metaphysical terms—as the space of *uwavi* (sorcery).

I never "discovered" *shikupi*.[4] I never transformed myself into a lion. I never stood at night in the village center, crying out that I saw sorcerers who fed on their neighbors and kin and that I would do away with them if they did not desist.[5] Kalamatatu saw, however, that the tools of my trade were pen and notebook, cassette recorder and camera. Perhaps he appreciated that one day I would write a book in which I would say of Muedans—including the sorcerers among them—what anthropologists generally do say: "I see you! I know who you are! I know what you're up to! I know what makes your world as it is!"[6] Kalamatatu might have recognized such claims as those of a sorcerer, for in my attempts to develop an ethnographic vision of *uwavi*, I—like Catholic missionaries and revolutionary socialists before me (West 2005a)—emulated the *muntela*'s (medicinal specialist) attempts to gain interpretative ascendancy in and over the world. Indeed, my argument that Muedan sorcery is, in the end, a "made thing" echoes the words of countersorcerers seeking to unmake and remake the world. Where Garro and Mattingly have suggested that the ethnographer seeks to be "a good storyteller of other people's stories" (2000: 29), Kalamatatu must have understood that every story potentially overturns (*kupilikula*) the stories it (re)tells. He "saw in me a kindred characteristic," I believe, because he knew that, in my writings, I would attempt to produce of the Muedan world an order of my own description—because he appreciated that such interpretative visions *of* the world necessarily constitute means of leverage *on* the world.[7]

Kalamatatu's conception of our collegial relationship may have implied not only that he considered me a (counter)sorcerer but also that he thought of himself as an ethnographer of sorts, for, again, his métier, like mine, entailed searching for the definitive logics of the world he studied. Kalamatatu might have agreed with Roy Wagner, who has argued that, because people—like the anthropologists who study them—construct rules, traditions, and social facts in order to make sense of societies (in which *they* actually *live*), everyone is a fieldworker of sorts, everyone an anthropologist (1975: 35). Taken together, Atanásio Herneo's conclusion that "everyone is a sorcerer," Wagner's, that everyone is an anthropologist, and the idea emerging from Kalamatatu's understandings of my work, and mine of his, that sorcery and ethnography are in many ways one and the same raise the question: Are we not all—to spawn a Shimakonde anthropological neologism—practitioners of *uwavi wa etinogalafia* (translatable as either "sorcery of ethnography" or "ethnographic sorcery")?

Of course, the sorcerer's interpretation of the world's workings is generally understood not only to undo (*kupilikula*) those preceding it but also to be vulnerable to being undone by those to follow. As a "made thing," the sorcerer's articulated vision is susceptible to being remade. If ethnographers and (counter)sorcerers are truly "colleagues," the same must be said of anthropological visions of the world.

Some would argue that anthropological inquiry is fundamentally different from the sorcerer's quest to understand his or her world.[8] Indeed, some would assert that anthropology constitutes a science whose methodology yields findings that indeed transcend the perspectives and understandings of the human condition held by the discipline's various native subjects. Others within the discipline itself would consider such claims as hubris. Clifford Geertz has famously argued: "Anthropological writings are themselves interpretations, and second or third order ones to boot. (By definition, only a 'native' makes first order ones: it's *his* culture.) They are, thus, fictions; fictions, in the sense that they are 'something made,' 'something fashioned'—the original meaning of *fictiō*—not that they are false, unfactual, or merely 'as if' thought experiments" (1973: 15). Not only did Geertz suggest that ethnographers' visions, like those of the Muedan sorcerer, are "made things," but he suggested, paraphrasing W. B. Gallie, that they are "essentially contestable" (Geertz 1973: 29). In the same spirit, Michael Jackson has concluded that we can "no longer assume that *our* texts have some kind of intrinsic epistemological superiority over *theirs*," because "[a]ll are, in the final consideration, metaphors, more or less masked, for an existential quest for meaning" (1989: 168).

Is such a stance sustainable? "Rationalists" (or, to use Geertz's term, "anti-relativists") have argued that any position accepting a multiplicity of incongruent truths is logically untenable, for it necessarily accepts as possible the conclusion that it is itself errant (Tambiah 1990: 128). Wagner, by contrast, has argued that "[t]he acid test of any anthropology is whether it is willing to apply . . . relativity *objectively*—to our 'reality' as well as to those of others—as well as *subjectively*." In accordance with his understanding that all cultures are the stuff of symbolic invention, he has written, "Unless we are able to *hold our own symbols responsible* for the reality we create with them, our notion of symbols and of culture in general will remain subject to the 'masking' by which our invention conceals its effects" (Wagner 1975: 144). The question remains, is it truly possible for the anthropologist—or anyone else for that matter—to conceive of his or her view of the world as fundamentally contestable?

I take inspiration in responding to the question from Muedans and their healers, who claimed to see the world's hidden, but definitive, workings while simultaneously admitting the limits of their abilities to do so. Where the former might be considered remarkable, the latter, I wish to suggest, may be even more so. Unlike Nick Jardine, who has asserted "there are certain vantage points to which we are forever tied by our humanity and hence cannot hope to transcend in our scientific theories" (1980: 24), Muedans told us that we humans can and do transcend our worldly perspectives (such maneuvers are, by definition, sorcery), even if only precariously. Indeed, Muedans asserted that we humans can scarcely avoid elaborating a vision of the world and its definitive workings—and seeing that vision, in time, replaced by another—for such is the stuff of life: one must inevitably formulate, articulate, and act within one's visions of the world, despite the ever-present threat of subsequent visions overturning one's own, for it is through such visions and countervisions that the world is actually made, unmade, and remade.

But what of this ethnographer's vision? Clearly, in suggesting that sorcery lions operated as "literal metaphors" or "embodied metaphors," I have made of Mueda and Muedans something that they themselves have not; I have remade them in accordance with my own vision. If so doing constitutes a form of sorcery, I am left to wonder—as did the dance troupe leader Fernando Chofer Nankoma—what kind of sorcerer I am. To what ends have I engaged with the Muedan life-world? What *have* I *made* of it, to return to the question as it was phrased earlier in this essay? Have I harmed, or have I healed? If, as Andras Sandor has told us, the power of metaphor depends upon reflection, have I fortified Muedans by facilitating reflection upon how they have made their world through imaginative flights of reference to the invisible realm of sorcery? Or have I—like Evans-Pritchard plucking charcoal from the witch doctor Bögwözu's poultice to expose him as a "fraud" ([1937] 1976: 103)—*dis*empowered Muedans by calling attention to the made-ness of their world and/or exposing *how* it has been made?

I would like to think that as I have narrated my encounter with Muedans and their sorcery-filled world here, and elsewhere—as I have elaborated my vision of that world for an audience that includes many with no other experience of it—I have challenged those before me who have portrayed Muedans, to their detriment, as ignorant, backward-looking, and primitive and that I have thus undone (*kupilikula*) such prejudicial gazes. I would like to think that I have persuaded my audience that, through the medium of sorcery discourse, Muedans have creatively interpreted and engaged with the historical events and processes shaping their world. I am left to hope that my work (*kudenga*) on, and in the space of, *uwavi* will be seen as a form of *uwavi wa kudenga* (sorcery of construction)[9]—that I will be judged to have engaged constructively with a world that I have shared (and continue to share) with Muedans.

Whereas postmodern critics might suggest that my interpretative vision of the Muedan life-world has "silenced" Muedans themselves, I dare say the Muedans with whom I worked expected me—like anyone else—to speak assertively and authoritatively, articulating as convincingly as I was able my vision of the world we shared. Muedans, it seemed to me, knew well what some critics of anthropology have been unable to grasp, namely, that *any* engagement with the world *requires* both the formulation of a vision (or "interpretation") and attempts to persuade one's fellows to conform to that vision (or to accept that interpretation)—even as that vision (or interpretation) is subjected to perpetual contestation and constant transformation.[10] (Those who do not articulate authoritative visions of the world are relegated, as Muedans often said, to sit at home and pick fleas from their feet.) Muedans with whom we worked were not inclined to treat my words or anyone else's as the last. In the sorcery-filled Muedan life-world we shared, every maneuver was the starting point for countermaneuver, every spin the stuff of counterspin, every interpretative vision the object of subsequent (re)visionings. Accordingly, any Muedans who "recognized" the power inherent in the ethnographer's transcendent vision implicitly asserted that *they* had managed to fix the anthropological seer in their own sights and, thus, to transcend *his* view. Not only has my vision been susceptible to challenge by those reading my published works and conducting fieldwork, after me, on the Mueda plateau, but it was and continues to be subjected to critique by Muedans themselves, who, by conceiving of me as a sorcerer, were already overturning (*kupilikula*) my perspectives and *remaking me* even as I worked among them.[11]

The Muedan life-world of which I write has made me as much as I will ever make it. As I have written about sorcery, I have spoken in terms mostly invented by others about a reality mostly made by them. Even as I have re-presented Muedan sorcery, I have not (re)made it at my whim. To the extent that I have (re)made the world I shared with Muedans, I have done so with great ambivalence, having learned from them the valuable lesson that, even as we necessarily (re)make the world in which we live, we do so at great risk to ourselves and to others. It is best, in such matters, to proceed cautiously, and with great humility.

Circular Arguments

Not to be a man, to be the projection of another man's dream, what a feeling of humiliation, of vertigo!
« JORGE LUIS BORGES, "The Circular Ruins" (1970: 77) »

I don't like belonging to another person's dream . . . I've a great mind to go and wake him, and see what happens!
« LEWIS CARROLL, *Through the Looking-Glass* ([1871] 1998: 205) »

As my 1999 research stint drew to a close, Marcos, Tissa, and I went one evening to visit with Terezinha "Mbegweka" António, assistant president of the Mueda branch of the Mozambican Traditional Medicine Association (Associação da Medicina Tradicional de Moçambique, or AMETRAMO). As we approached her house, we met branch president João Chombo in the road, walking toward Mbegweka's. Chombo, who normally lived in the lowland village of Nanyala, stayed at Mbegweka's when in Mueda on AMETRAMO business. We continued toward Mbegweka's together.

Chombo had been drinking, making him more animated and assertive than usual. He told us that he had returned late that afternoon from the South African–owned lumber camp on the Mueda–Mocímboa da Praia road at the plateau's eastern edge.

"The Boers invited me there," he told us. "They wanted me to treat their camp."

"Have they had problems there?" I asked.

"Ah, where there is wealth, there are always problems," he answered. He went on to tell us that he had discovered the presence of a *lindandosho* in the camp. "There was an owl in the office building that someone had put there to steal money," he explained.[1]

"Did you take care of it?" I asked.

"No," he answered. "The Boers wouldn't let me in the office, so it's still in there."

We arrived in Mbegweka's yard, where we were greeted. We sat together while Mbegweka attended to a patient before joining us.

Chombo turned to me and spoke with intensity. "The trouble with these Boers is that they think they are different from other people just because they are white. They think that they don't have problems with *uwavi* because they aren't black."

"Is that why they refused to let you deal with the owl?" I asked.

"Yes," he answered. "They didn't let me vaccinate them either." Chombo shook his head. "Foolish Boers!" He added, with agitation, "They will suffer for this."

I imagined that the South Africans who had summoned Chombo to the lumber camp had hoped to use him to frighten their workers and other potential thieves. But Chombo had proved an unwieldy instrument in their hands. He had turned attention on them, on their exceptionalism, and on their disbelief in the very force they hoped others believed in. They had got what was coming to them, I thought to myself. I smiled and nodded affirmingly as Chombo repeated his condemnation: "Foolish Boers!"

I immediately realized that, at that very moment, I used Chombo too—as a foil to the manipulations of South African entrepreneurs arriving in large numbers in post–civil war, postsocialist Mozambique. How was I any different from them,

I wondered? I was relieved when the topic of conversation changed.

Chombo now turned to Marcos and began to tell another story. Only two nights before, he had been working with a patient here in Mbegweka's yard when a drunk stumbled in. As it turned out, the drunk was the elder brother of the man he was treating. The drunk asked Chombo to treat him as well, but Chombo told him that he did not work on people when they were intoxicated. The man insisted, and Chombo again refused. A scuffle ensued, and the man was expelled from the yard. The next morning, he was found lying dead in the roadway nearby. Later that day, Chombo told us, the younger brother committed suicide after being accused of killing the older brother with sorcery.

Chombo now thrust his elbow in front of Marcos for inspection. "There is where I was injured," he said, pointing to a small cut. "I am no *mwavi*," he added, as he leaned back against the wall of Mbegweka's house. "But these men attacked me, and the next day they were dead." He looked to the ground and, then, after a pause, pointed his finger in front of him, saying, "I am João Chombo, president of Mueda!"

Chombo did not bother to qualify his statement to indicate that he was president only of the district healers association, for perhaps he considered his power as such to eclipse all other offices. Marcos let out a ribald laugh. Tissa joined in with nervous rolling laughter. I sat silently, wondering where the conversation might lead. Chombo was completely uninhibited. His every word accentuated the fine line between constructive and destructive power. He seemed to derive satisfaction from the ambiguity in which he cloaked himself. I found myself eager to once more underscore my friendship with him. I told him of our plans for a feast the next day, at Mbegweka's, to show our gratitude for the assistance that he and his healers association had rendered us. He explained that he had to travel at the break of dawn to treat a patient in a village in the lowlands northeast of the plateau and that he would be unable to attend the feast.

We sat quietly for a few moments. Then Chombo leaned forward and grasped my hand. "We have worked well together, Andiliki," he now said. His grip was firm. "I cannot let you travel without vaccinating you against the dangers that surround you."[2]

My heart quickened. During my years working with healers, I had submitted to all manner of treatments. I had inhaled vapors. Pastes had been rubbed on my skin. I had ingested various substances. Packets of *mitela* had been tied around my limbs, around my neck, and around my waist. But now, the moment I had long dreaded was upon me. "Vaccination"—the slitting of the skin with a razor blade and the insertion in the incision of *mitela*, generally mixed with the acid of a disposable battery—was the one Muedan treatment I feared.

I tried to focus my thoughts—to still the panic welling up inside me. Of all people, the offer came from Chombo—"the most powerful healer on the Mueda plateau." I quickly realized from his tone that Chombo expected me to resist. Even as he told us about the other resistant patients—the "foolish" South African lumber-camp managers—with whom he had recently worked, Chombo had intended to vaccinate me, I realized. He had ensured that I understood that there were serious consequences to my decision. At the very least, I realized, I could not preserve the friendship I had with him if I "refused" his treatment. A rupture with him would be disastrous, I thought, even as I was about to leave the plateau, for how could I claim any "understanding" with Muedan *vakulaula* if, in my final days of fieldwork, I fell out with their president? How could I claim to speak sensibly about Muedan sorcery knowing my mutual trust with the most respected of all Muedan countersorcerers had been broken?

Fortunately, Chombo was restless. Suddenly, he was talking about other things. He asked me if I could buy a vehicle for him. Then he said, abruptly, "Take me to America."

During our time working together, Marcos had become quite adept at shielding me from such requests. He now took up the case as I sat quietly thinking about how to avoid vaccination.

"Chombo," he said, playfully but assertively. "Do you know how much it costs to travel to America?"

"Ahhhh, I don't care!" he retorted. "If he can buy a ticket for himself, he can buy one for me!"

"He's never bought one for me," Marcos said, "and I've been working with him for years."

"Well," Chombo said, "have you asked?"

They laughed together. My mind raced.

"Anyway, he doesn't buy the tickets. It's the school he works for that buys them. He doesn't have that much money."

"Well, he can tell *them* to buy me a ticket," Chombo responded.

"Why would they want to bring you to America?" Marcos asked. "You can't even read or write."

"I know many things," Chombo reminded Marcos. "I know how to heal terrible diseases that no one in America knows how to heal. America needs to know what João Chombo knows!" he thundered.

Marcos reached out for Chombo's hand to clasp it in affirmation of the truth in his words. Then he said, quietly, "Chombo, do you know how long it takes to travel to America?"

Chombo admitted that he did not.

"Do you remember those jets that flew over us during the *luta* [the war for Mozambican independence]?"

Chombo pointed to the sky and nodded affirmatively.

"To travel to America, you have to get in one of those," Marcos said. "You can't get there in a car, and you can't get there in a bus, and you can't get there in a train. You can't even get there in a helicopter. It's too far."

Chombo listened patiently.

"Do you know how long it takes in one of those jets?" Marcos asked him.

"How long?" he responded.

"Three weeks," Marcos said, apparently thinking that the twenty-four hours or so of airtime that he knew it actually took would be insufficient to prove his point. I considered correcting him but remained too preoccupied with finding a way to rescue myself from vaccination.

"Do you know how much you have to take with you on a journey like that?"

Chombo now looked impressed.

"Think about all the sacks of corn meal and rice, and all the water you have to carry."

"Hmmm," Chombo said, absorbing the details of the picture Marcos painted. "Perhaps it isn't possible," he concluded. "It would be very expensive for my friend here to arrange all of that."[3]

Although Chombo was now convinced that he would never travel to America, Marcos had set me to thinking about Chombo's desire to share his knowledge with America and Americans. I realized that my salvation might lie in this. I began to speak, even as thoughts were forming in my head, even as I formulated a new language with which to convey a novel perspective I hoped Chombo would share with me.

"Chombo," I said, "I have learned during my time in Mueda that people have different ways of seeing the world and different ways of acting in the world. Some *vakulaula* see the world through dreams. Others see it through the words of ancestral spirits. Others use *mitela*. Some even have *shikupi,* so that they can see *vavi* at night."

Chombo hummed in agreement.

"Well, I see the world through the stories that people share with me. I gather stories the way that *vakulaula* gather *mitela*."

Chombo nodded.

I grew more hopeful.

"There are 'founders' who invent their own *mitela,*" I continued, "but most *mitela* is learned from others. Stories, like *mitela,* often come from someone else. I have learned most of my stories from others."

Again, Chombo hummed.

"When I return to America, I will tell people there what I have learned. I will tell the stories that have been told to me.

I will write these stories down in books that people will read. And always, I will say whose stories they are."

I now looked Chombo in the eye.

"People in America and elsewhere will know what João Chombo has told me. They will know what João Chombo knows because I will tell them what you have told me."

Chombo now reached for my hand and shook it firmly.

"Thank you," he said. "Thank you very much."

I was not yet safe from vaccination, I knew. I drew breath and continued.

"Chombo," I said, "I have also learned that *vakulaula* do not use their *mitela* only to heal. They also use it to protect against harm before it happens."

"Yes," he said, focused on my words.

"Well, as I have traveled the plateau, I have used my stories in the same way. Everywhere that I have gone, I have told people that I work here among the *vakulaula* of Mueda with the permission of João Chombo, president of AMETRAMO-Mueda. Everyone knows that I travel with your approval. Everyone knows that I work with your blessing."

"You do," Chombo said.

I was now close to my conclusion. I knew that Chombo might as easily laugh at me as agree with what I was about to say. I carried on nonetheless.

"Your blessing on my work and the knowledge that you have shared with me . . . I carry these things with me wherever I go."

"It is true," he said, shaking my hand.

"You told me once that if you gave me your *mitela*, I could not use it because I didn't know how to use it. You told me that the power lies not in *mitela* but in knowledge."[4]

Chombo turned to Marcos and said, of me, *"Andimanya"* (He knows).

"I know that your blessing and your wisdom go with me to America, even if you don't vaccinate me. Because I know that your power lies in your knowledge, I feel that you have *already treated me* by sharing a bit of that knowledge with me. So, I don't feel like I need to be vaccinated."

Chombo now looked at me, still holding my hand firmly and shaking it. After what seemed to me an eternal pause, he said, "*Undimanya* [You know], Andiliki."

I held tight my breath for fear that, if I let loose the sigh within me, I would somehow betray myself. I hoped to get away as soon as I could, before Chombo changed his mind—before he sifted through the hocus-pocus of my words, before he inverted them, undid them, annulled them (*kupilikula*).

"It is late, and you will be traveling tomorrow," I said. "We should go now and let you sleep."

Chombo wished me a good journey and asked when I would return. I told him that I didn't know when, but that I would see him again.

Marcos and Tissa lingered with Chombo as Mbegweka escorted me to the edge of her yard. I had declined Chombo's offer, but Marcos and Tissa scrambled in the aftermath of my words to take the most powerful healer in Mueda up on his offer to vaccinate.

The next morning, they rose just before sunrise and returned to Mbegweka's yard. They awakened Mbegweka only to find that Chombo had left for the lowlands under cover of darkness, when only "those without fear" travel.

Notes

PREFACE

1. The description that Christopher Davis provides of Tabwa "'magical' circumstantial therapies" as the production of "analogous worlds . . . fitted together like so many *concentric circles*" (2000: 300, emphasis added) similarly resonates with Borges's "Circular Ruins."

MISUNDERSTANDING

1. When I told Muedans that my English name, Harry, could be translated into Portuguese as Henrique, they informed me that, in Shimakonde, Henrique was pronounced Andiliki. Many Muedans in fact bear the "Shimakonde name" Andiliki, while others (generally more literate) call themselves Henrique in "proper Portuguese."

2. See also Sarró 2000: 179.

IN SEARCH OF THE FORWARD-LOOKING PEASANT

1. On this point, see M. F. Brown 1986: 15; Ciekawy and Geschiere 1998: 1; Hallen 2001: 80.

2. See also Bond and Ciekawy 2001: 1–5.

3. On other occasions, it was explained to me that sorcery lions were also identified by unusual behavior, such as lingering near human settlements (West 2005a: xxiii, xxvi, xxvii–xxviii). In reference to Evans-Pritchard's accounts of Nuer statements that "twins are birds" and similar ideas among Tikopia, Raymond Firth has noted, "A bird that behaves normally is 'just a bird'" (1966: 10).

4. In this regard, Muedans acted like the *benandanti* of sixteenth-and seventeenth-century Italy, who intuitively understood that commentary on the lived experience of witchcraft was appropriate to some sociopolitical contexts and not to others (Ginsburg [1966] 1992: 83).

5. In this regard, my experience was similar to that of Clyde Kluckhohn (1944: 14), who studied Navaho witchcraft in the 1940s. See also Favret-Saada 1980: 77; Tannenbaum 1993: 67.

6. See also Ciekawy 1998: 120.

"THIS MUST BE STUDIED SCIENTIFICALLY"

1. Mair (1969: 199–221) offered a useful summary of such approaches, while Dillon-Malone (1988) has provided a more contemporary example of the approach, replete with statistics on the frequencies of occurrence of accusations directed at specific categories of people. See also Forde 1958: 170.

2. In his work on Navaho witchcraft, Kluckhohn (1944) also asserted that those accused of witchcraft were generally the elderly, the wealthy, and the powerful. More recently, Ciekawy (Ciekawy and Geschiere 1998: 128) and Niehaus (2001: 198) have identified the aged as primary targets of sorcery/witchcraft accusations in Kenya and in South Africa, respectively.

3. Beidelman (1963: 74) also identified outsiders and co-wives as among common witchcraft suspects. Mombeshora (1994: 71) has more recently argued that witchcraft is a "smoke-screen for generational conflicts embedded in the social fabric of kinship and marriage," while Rodman (1993) has argued that emergent postcolonial elites are most often accused by villagers seeking to level social disparities.

4. Cf. Niehaus (Niehaus, Mohlala, and Shokane 2001: 83–112), who has argued that, while witchcraft accusations *can* be read as indices of social strain, the vectors of accusation are multiple and contradictory.

5. See also Lambek 1993: 238; Whyte 1997: 200.

6. An *igoli* is a knee-high platform made of a braided reed cord lattice stretched over a rectangular wooden frame and elevated from the ground by four wooden legs. It may serve as a bed or as a bench on which to sit.

BELIEF AS METAPHOR

1. See also Lewis 1994: 569.

2. See also Ashforth 2000: 244–245.

3. Sister Rosa Carla's dismissal of sorcery as superstition contrasts greatly with the approach taken to European forms of witchcraft and sorcery by the church during the Inquisition, when such forces were generally conceived of as the work of the devil (Ginzburg [1966] 1992), as well as with that of many contemporary Protestant sects in Africa. Sister Rosa Carla's response bears evidence of the partial (sometimes paradoxical) historical penetration of Catholicism by a scientific worldview.

4. Notwithstanding his ambivalence about anthropology as a "science," as Tambiah has told us, "Evans-Pritchard did subscribe to the notion that there was a context-independent notion of 'reality' (the 'reality' whose truth 'science' establishes) against which the rationality of Zande notions of witchcraft and oracles could be judged and be found wanting" (Tambiah 1990: 117). He even wrote: "Witches, as the Azande conceive them, clearly cannot exist" (Evans-Pritchard 1965: 18). Abrahams similarly concluded that beliefs in witchcraft were "mistaken" (1994: 11). Bailey, borrowing a phrase from Ibsen, suggested that witchcraft/sorcery beliefs constituted "lies that make life possible" (1994: 4). It should be noted that Evans-Pritchard's position on such matters changed subtly after he embraced Catholicism later in life. According to Engelke, "Evans-Pritchard stopped just short of saying a background as a believer gives the anthropologist a privileged understanding [of religious experience]" (2002: 6). Albeit still asserting a "scientific perspective," Evans-Pritchard himself wrote that "there is no possibility of [the anthropologist's] knowing whether the spiritual beings of primitive religions or of any others have any existence or not, and since that is the case he cannot take the question into consideration. The beliefs are for him sociological facts, not theological facts, and his sole concern is with their relation to other social facts. His problems are scientific, not merely metaphysical or ontological" (1965: 17).

5. Here, "science" connotes something different than it did in my discussions with Marcos in the preceding chapter. Those conversations were about the sociological patterns of sorcery. These are about the truth of claims that people actually make or become lions.

6. See also Plotkin 1993: 101–102, 230–231, 266–267.

7. See also Willis and Chisanga 1999. Willis has claimed to have seen spirits, to have been attacked by sorcerers, and to have himself healed people while conducting fieldwork in Zambia. Whereas Stoller has been accused by some of having "gone native," Willis—who claimed to have been married in a prior life to "the same entity who

later became Mary Magdalene" (9)—has spoken of his own healing career not as a product of his anthropological fieldwork exclusively but, instead, as a life trajectory that has sometimes intersected with his anthropological fieldwork.

8. See also Beattie 1970: 261.

9. See also Pels 1999: 275. Pels has similarly argued that Luguru accounts of *mumiani* (bloodsuckers) can be read as a metaphorical commentary on extractive colonial relations.

10. On belief as metaphor, see also Auge 1975; Bailey 1994: 39, 85, 106; Beattie 1964; Boddy 1989: 337–360; de Heusch 1985; Fernandez 1991: 218; Firth 1966; Laderman 1991: 13; Leach 1964; Lévi-Strauss 1966; Pitt-Rivers 1970: 187; Ruel 1970: 334; Sahlins 1981; Schmoll 1993: 205; Stoller and Olkes 1987: 229; Tambiah 1985. Ashforth (1998) and Willis (Willis and Chisanga 1999: 115) have explicitly conceived of animal familiars as metaphors.

11. Horton has rather cynically concluded that most symbolists are motivated by "a deep sense of guilt and anxiety about the arrogantly invidious comparisons made by their predecessors between the thought of the West and that of the non-West" (1993: 135). He has written: "Most Symbolists accept that non-Western world-views, *if* considered as systems for explanation, prediction and control, and *if* measured as such against the yardstick of modern Western science, emerge as markedly inferior to the latter. By denying that explanation, prediction and control are the *real* aims of non-Western religious discourse, Symbolists are able to satisfy their liberal scruples" (7; see also 58–61, 128). Horton cites Barley, who once sarcastically concluded: "It looks crazy. It must be symbolism" (128).

12. Langford (2002: 200) has suggested that, in similar fashion, medical anthropologists often forgo evaluation of a practice's biological efficacy in favor of examining its symbolic efficacy.

13. Cf. Jackson 1989: 107–108.

"THE PROBLEM MAY LIE THERE"

1. *Likola* is the term for a Makonde matrilineage; a *likola* sister is a mother's sister's daughter, who is treated by Makonde as a sibling.

2. On 16 June 1960, colonial police fired on a crowd of demonstrators in Mueda town. The incident—subsequently referred to by Mozambican nationalists as the "Mueda Massacre"—was celebrated as the precipitating event in the struggle for Mozambican independence.

3. In the run-up to the 1994 elections, through which the peace was consolidated after the 1977–1992 Mozambican civil war, the UN established demobilization centers throughout the country where government or rebel troops were disarmed, quartered, and prepared for reintegration into civilian life.

4. Despite buying my vehicle through a contact made via a Ford dealership in Pretoria, I later discovered that it had, at some point in its brief life, had its VIN (vehicle identification number) changed—a sure sign that it was once stolen.

5. Green (1994: 35) has described Pogoro antiwitchcraft rites that also involve painting the subject's head with a cross.

WHOSE METAPHORS?

1. Joanna Overing has written: "It is easier for us to accept the poetic informant than to accept (even intellectually) a person who claims to believe what is totally crazy, untrue and irrational according to our own empirically based truth conditions and formal rules of logic" (1985: 152).

2. See also Hallen and Sodipo 1986: 7–8.

3. See also Weiner 1994: 597–598.

4. Evans-Pritchard famously argued, with regard to the Nuer metaphor "twins are birds," that "Nuer are not saying that a twin is like a bird but that he is a bird" (1956: 131). Nonetheless, he asserted that, depending upon the content and context of Nuer metaphors, "is" may have various connotations ranging from the identity of one entity with another to the manifestation of one entity in another. He concluded that it would be a mistake to discount the "poetic sense" expressed in Nuer metaphors (142). See also Lienhardt 1954: 97–98 (where it is suggested that such statements lie between the literal and the figurative); and commentary on Evans-Pritchard and on Lienhardt in Firth 1966. Atkinson, following Castaneda ([1968] 1990), has told us that only with time did she come to appreciate that her Wana informants "treated aspects of 'non-ordinary reality'—not 'as if' they were real, but rather 'as real'" (1989: 37). See also Hsu 1999: 212. Townsley (1997: 14–15) has pointed out that it is often impossible analytically to discern whether people "believe" the metaphors they use. In any case, Muedans with whom we worked did not assert that Imbwambwe was *like* a lion but rather that he *was* a lion. See also Whitehead 2002: 97.

5. Firth argued: "Belief in the existence of men-lions rests not only on abstract perception of contrast and resolution of opposites but also on concrete experiences of anxiety, terror and destruction" (1966: 3). See also Ciekawy and Geschiere 1998: 3.

6. Hollis has warned against trying to figure out what beliefs such as Azande witchcraft are "about," for, to Azande, they are about nothing other than witchcraft (1970: 226). See also Ellis and ter Haar 1998: 186; Hastrup 1995: 33; Overing 1985: 158; Palmié 2002: 3; Peel 1969. Cf. Lattas 1993: 68; Simmons 1980.

7. Luhrmann (1989), by contrast, has described witches in contemporary England who themselves sometimes characterize their own "beliefs" as metaphorical.

8. Horton (1993: 110) would agree with this and, for that reason, would suggest that there is no metaphor, or symbol, here but only an errant attempt at explanation. His conclusion, he argues, demonstrates less arrogance than symbolist defenses of failed logical thinking through suggestions that such thought is "really about" something else.

9. This is not to suggest that Muedans, or other Africans, never self-reflexively deploy metaphor. Indeed, symbolists have often suggested that they do so even within the context of ritual expression of religious "belief." See, e.g., de Heusch 1985 on the use of metaphor in sacrifice. See also Devisch 1990 and Joralemon and Sharon 1993: 246–256 on the explicit use of metaphorical statements—recognized by healers and patients as such—in the practices of Yaka healers (in Zaire) and Peruvian *curanderos,* respectively. See also Tambiah 1969 and Urton 1985 on the explicit use of animals as metaphors for social relations.

POWERS OF PERSPECTIVE AND PERSUASION

1. Langford (2002: 188–230) has given a fascinating account of similar conversations she had with those among whom she worked regarding the authenticity/fraudulence of healing practices.

2. Atkinson (1989: 75) has suggested that, among Wana, the force of magic depends both upon its operations being kept secret *and* upon the revelation to others that magic has been made. Taussig has proposed that "revelation is precisely what the secret intends" (1998: 242).

3. Whitehead (2002: 11–40) has given an account of a similar experience. See also Rasmussen 2001: xvi. Cf. Favret-Saada 1980: 18,

where she suggests that it is difficult for the investigator to occupy the vulnerable space of the bewitched.

MAKING MEANING, MAKING THE WORLD

1. See also Firth 1966: 15.

2. Wittgenstein similarly argued: "All testing, all confirmation and disconfirmation of a hypothesis takes place within a system. . . . The system is not so much the point of departure as the element in which arguments have their life" (in Tambiah 1990: 64). Winch, following Wittgenstein, wrote: "Reality is not what gives language sense. What is real and what is unreal shows itself in the sense that language has" (1970: 82). Along the same lines, Voloshinov suggested that "language is constitutive of human experience," according to Todorov (1984: 29). "There is no experience outside its embodiment in signs. . . . It is not experience that organizes expression, but, to the contrary, expression that organizes experience. . . . Outside material expression, no experience. More, expression precedes experience, it is its cradle" (Voloshinov in Todorov 1984: 43). Following Bakhtin and Voloshinov, Williams (1977: 21–44) argued for the need to treat language as a constitutive material activity rather than as a means of expressing understandings of an a priori reality. See also Lee 1959: 8; Whorf 1956.

3. See also Hallen and Sodipo's discussion of Yoruba witchcraft in light of the writings of the philosopher W. V. O. Quine, who "prefers to regard each natural language . . . as a unique and complex theory for describing experience that conveys its own ontology, which may be distinct from that of any other," and who argues, according to Hallen and Sodipo: "Immediate experience does not 'present itself' as ordered and categorized. It is man, with his language and the theories he uses it to construct . . . who defines meaning and order" (Hallen and Sodipo 1986: **16**).

4. Gottlieb has provided further evidence that through such discursive formations, people may perceive themselves as makers of their own world; a Beng Master of the Earth once told her, "My religion is powerful, it is real, but it is we who create it. Without our faith, it does not exist. Our gods are our invention" (Gottlieb 1992: 44). Davis has asserted that "'magical' circumstantial therapy" (the term she uses for healing among Tabwa) similarly "takes the same form as godliness and, in so far as they are able, human beings control life by standing as god in relation to themselves and their world" (C. O. Davis 2000: 300).

5. See also Atkinson 1989: 16, 37–39; M. F. Brown 1986: 50; Humphrey 1996: 76; Lattas 1993; Stoller 1989: 14.

MASKED AND DANGEROUS

1. Israel (2005; forthcoming) has conducted extensive research on masquerade in the Mueda plateau region and reports that this dance, called *nshindo,* is a genre of the *mapiko* masquerade with which Makonde residents of the Mueda plateau region are closely associated. His research has demonstrated that *nshindo,* which literally means "foot stamping," arose in the late 1940s in the lowlands around the Messalo River.

2. This was just under $4 at the time.

3. According to Israel's research (forthcoming), the fact that *nshindo* was performed at funerals contributed to its historical disappearance on the plateau itself, where colonial-era missionaries condemned such practices as heathen. Israel also reports that in the wake of Catholic evangelization, plateau residents set aside this genre of masquerade due to its depiction of sorcery.

4. See Dias and Dias 1970: 391–393. Bortolot (forthcoming) has recently conducted research on masquerade in the Mueda region and writes that the secret of the *lipiko's* identity has long been a public one.

5. See also Bortolot, forthcoming; Dias and Dias 1970: 200; Israel, forthcoming.

6. This *nshindo* performance differed somewhat from the norm, perhaps owing to my having commissioned it. For a description of the typical *nshindo* performance, see Israel, forthcoming.

7. Israel (forthcoming) explains that the *nshindo* genre of masquerade generally includes this kind of theatrical component, although no word exists in Shimakonde to differentiate it from the dance.

8. A *capulana* is a rectangular printed cloth, worn by women as a wrap skirt but also serving dozens of other functions.

9. Historically, *lipiko* have represented spiritual entities (Dias and Dias 1970: 391–393). According to Israel (forthcoming), other entities were also represented by *lipiko* masks in the *nshindo* genre, including Ngoni fishermen (present in the region), Masaai warriors (whom Makonde might have encountered while in Tanzania), and Germans (who passed through the region during World War I and who owned sisal plantations in the region thereafter). By his account, the character of the sorcerer dates to the introduction of a mask in the 1950s that

represented an individual widely suspected of having been a sorcerer. According to Israel, this reinforced prior associations of *nshindo* with sorcery; *nshindo* in fact derived from *mapiko a shilo,* a genre dating to the 1930s that was widely associated with sorcery because it was danced at night and used masks representing animals and dangerous spirits.

10. Whitehead (2002: 169) has offered a similar account of healers treating dark sorcerers made sick by their consumption of victims.

11. Whether sorcerer or not, the *lipiko* and his dancing by all accounts produced an atmosphere conducive to sorcery. According to Bortolot (forthcoming): "*Mapiko* performers, dancing alone at the center of crowds of people animated by emotions of competition, pride, and jealousy, are left completely exposed to all manner of unseen attacks. . . . By laying themselves open to attack, the actors involved essentially 'call out' those who would engage in such antisocial behaviors and demonstrate their knowledge of *uwavi* by effectively protecting themselves against them. . . . People say that during performances the air is thick with *uwavi,* and anyone who stands out from the crowd may get caught, quite literally, in the crossfire." (Bortolot has written that he in fact fell violently ill the day after filming a performance from the elevated perspective of a chair.) Israel (forthcoming) has reported that *nshindo* performers "mine" the enclosure in which they perform with antisorcery *mitela* and sometimes post a healer at its opening to mitigate these dangers.

12. According to Israel (forthcoming), *nshindo* performers themselves often speak of their performance as an "antisorcery dance" rather than a "sorcery dance."

13. Israel (forthcoming) has reported that dancers are instructed in how to portray sorcery by elders who often are countersorcery healers; where this is the case, he suggests, the question is one of how these elders know what sorcery looks like without having undertaken it.

14. Stoller has similarly suggested that Songhay spirit possession, as theatrical performance, constitutes "a deliberate attack on reality but for the transformation of life" (1989: 209–210). Kingdon has suggested that the ritual unmasking of *mapiko* in the context of male initiation rites itself constituted a "revelation" of the "true . . . cosmological order"; in other words, it revealed the existence of that which it represented (2002: 49). Elsewhere, he has offered fascinating commentary on the way that Makonde sculpture has, similarly, mediated

between "experiential realms," producing images of things at once "not quite known" and "not quite unknown" and, ultimately, affording "astonishing disclosure[s] of a frightening ontological incompleteness" (2002: 146, 199).

15. Bortolot has reported that, in the village of Matambalale, practitioners of another dance genre, *mang'anyamu* (in which dancers dress in animal skins), were similarly suspected by fellow villagers of practicing sorcery and that they similarly responded with ambivalence, "[taking] these rumors very seriously, while also finding them somewhat empowering" (personal communication, 16 November 2005). According to Israel (n.d.), this genre had long been considered an innocuous, playful dance, but within the context of a spate of lion maulings in 2002–2003, the dance was interpreted as more sinister.

ARTICULATED VISIONS

1. Individuals claiming to be sorcerers were, in fact, generally dismissed as insane.

2. See also Middleton 1963: 266.

3. Sefu's words are reminiscent of Sandombu's in Victor Turner's classic ethnography *Schism and Continuity* ([1957] 1996: 95, 118)— words that ended in his being expelled temporarily from his village and barred from becoming chief. Marwick described Chewa convictions that sorcerers could be detected by their "threatening and prophetic language" (1967: 107). The threat of sorcery, like sorcery accusations, was often veiled in euphemism in Mueda, as elsewhere (see also Mair 1969: 219; Whyte 1997: 31). Middleton has asserted that, among Lugbara, the euphemism "You will see me later" was understood by all as a threat (1967: 58). Chavunduka has told us that, in Shona, "We shall meet" is considered to be a sorcerer's threat (1978: 17). Scott has argued that euphemism provides a way of making political statements with which regnant powers have difficulty dealing (1990: 152–154). Fisiy has provided evidence of this in his account of a Cameroonian legal research project that debated whether or not the euphemism "You shall see!" could be considered a threat in a court of law (1998: 147).

4. Boddy has similarly referred to Zār healing rituals as "metasocial" and "metacultural" productions (1989: 9). Van der Geest and Whyte (1989: 361) have argued that metaphors and metonyms are used to render illness concrete and, thus, treatable by concrete inter-

ventions. See also Luedke 2005. On the place of rhetoric in "symbolic healing," see Kirkmayer 1993: 163.

5. See also Fadiman 1993; Middleton and Winter 1963: 21; Thompson 1982.

6. Geschiere (1997) has argued, along similar lines, that witchcraft may be understood to operate as a force favoring either social differentiation or the leveling of social difference; see also Fisiy and Geschiere 1991; cf. Kluckhohn 1944: 118–121; Lattas 1993: 52; Middleton and Winter 1963: 13.

7. See also Beattie 1963: 51–52; Fadiman 1993; Thomas 1970: 67–68.

8. See also Bongmba 2001: 54; Evans-Pritchard [1937] 1976: 54; Green 1994: 27. In such cases, sorcery discourse may be said to act as a "hidden transcript" of resistance, to use James Scott's (1990) terminology.

9. See also Bond and Ciekawy 2001: 14; Crawford [1967] 1970: 323–324.

10. See also Bastian 2003; Bongmba 1998: 178; Devisch 2001: 119; Goheen 1996: 146; Sanders 2001: 170.

11. Ardener has told us that, among Bakweri in West Cameroon in the late colonial period, the relatively more prosperous were widely suspected of having built their tin-roofed homes with zombie slave labor (1970: 147–148).

12. See also Bayart 1993: 248–249; Goheen 1996: 160–161. Geschiere (1997: 113) has argued that such accusations may have negative repercussions for the accusers insofar as they may drive elites away from the village permanently, foreclosing all possibility of the sharing of wealth. See also Fisiy 1998: 146; Fisiy and Geschiere 2001: 236; Geschiere and Nyamnjoh 1998: 81–82.

13. Cf. Bastian (2001), who has described the confessions of teenage prostitute witches in Nigeria who claimed to have rendered their business-class clients economically impotent. Through such confessions, these young women not only "criticized" the destructive acts that they themselves perpetrated but also, arguably, produced restraining anxieties among the category of people they claimed to have acted against.

14. I give greater detail of this elsewhere (West forthcoming); see also the account provided by Israel (n.d.), who was conducting research in the district at the time of these events.

BRIDGING DOMAINS

1. Compare this with cases in the ethnographic literature on "lion-people" and/or "leopard-people" in which ethnographers and/or those among whom they have worked have suggested that people "dress up" as such beasts to attack their victims (for example, donning boxing gloves with knives protruding from the knuckles to produce the effects of an animal attack). In some instances, "lion societies" or "leopard societies" reportedly have "assassinated" their enemies in such disguise. See, e.g., Ellis 1999; Kalous 1974; Lindskog 1954; MacCormick 1983; Parsons [1927] 1970: 235–236; Pratten 2002; Pratten, forthcoming; Roberts 1986; Shaw 2001.

2. This was the line I sometimes took in my conversations with Marcos, simultaneously suggesting that the rising occurrence of lion-sorcery corresponded either with the movement of populations into previously unsettled areas or with the onset of the rainy season, which brought wild animals up from the lowlands to the plateau (West 2005a: xxviii).

3. Basso has argued that "the production and interpretation of metaphorical speech" entails "an ability to form novel semantic categories" (1976: 95). Here I argue that Muedans produced and inhabited novel ontological domains.

4. Lee similarly concluded: "Symbol is in fact a part of the whole, a component of the field which also contains the so-called *thing*, as well as the process of symbolizing, and the apprehending individual" (1959: 79).

5. "Metaphor is not simply a mapping of similarities from one domain to another; it creates similarities by demanding that we construct a category or a world in which connections between topic and vehicle can be found" (Kirkmayer 1993: 172).

6. This is, perhaps, the same *bridge* that Eliade (1964: 482) suggested shamans must cross in their healing rites.

7. On "embodied metaphor," see also Low 1994.

8. Garro and Mattingly (2000: 11–12) have similarly argued that healers' narratives do not merely reflect a world outside them but they also do something in that world. In his ethnography of Aguaruna magic, Michael Brown (1986: 25) has asserted the need to recognize a link between symbolization and its material effects, giving ontological precedence to neither. See also Lambek 1993: 291–293; Plotkin 1993: 262; Townsley 1997: 17.

9. Kirkmayer has made the same point, telling us that the metaphor "surgeons are butchers" may color how we think about the former in substantial ways (1992: 332).

10. Turner similarly suggested that ritual operates in a "subjunctive mood" (1981: 159).

WORKING WITH INDETERMINACY

1. This is not to suggest that Muedans read the Mozambican "transition to democracy" only through the discourse of sorcery. Elsewhere, I have argued that Muedans simultaneously engaged with the world through a variety of (sometimes complementary and sometimes contradictory) discursive formations (West 2005a).

2. According to Rosenthal (1998: 201), Ewe similarly conceive of Voodoo as an unwieldy power.

3. Goody reported that the death of Gonja chiefs was always assumed to be due to witchcraft, as "it [was] only a matter of time" before one of a chief's many witch enemies discovered an exploitable weakness (1970: 228).

4. See also Favret-Saada 1980: 122.

5. See also Beidelman 1993: 4, 206; Gottlieb 1992: 14.

6. See also Jackson 1996: 30.

7. See also Favret-Saada 1980: 13; Palmié 2002.

8. Fernandez too has suggested that metaphors may "edify . . . by puzzlement" ([1982] 1986: 222): "Symbolic productions speak to that inchoate condition, at once providing us with images which we can perform so as to act our way through those intense moments in life (the sacred ones—in which dilemmas, ambiguities and problems ultimately unresolvable threaten to overwhelm us); while at the same time they expand our awareness and temper our intolerance for such incongruities and incompatibilities" (223). Rosalind Shaw (1991) has similarly attributed the power of divination (a component of Muedan sorcery) to its "cryptic potency."

9. Philip Peek has argued: "Many African peoples maintain that 'real' knowledge is hidden, secret, available only to certain people capable of using it properly" (1991: 14). Francis Nyamnjoh has suggested: "If the reality of politics were limited to the apparent and the transparent as prescribed by liberal democracy, there would hardly be reason to explain success or failure otherwise. In general, if people had what they merited, and merited what they had in liberal democratic

terms, there would be little need for a hidden hand of any kind, real or imagined. But because nothing is what it seems, the invisible must be considered to paint a full picture of reality" (2001: 37).

10. See also Ciekawy and Geschiere 1998; Meyer 1998.

11. Whereas Evans-Pritchard ([1937] 1976: 65) argued that Azande did not constantly worry themselves about witchcraft, Muedans did worry constantly about the operation of power, whether in the visible or the invisible realm. In this regard, they acted more like Madumo, as described in Ashforth 2000.

12. In a similar vein, whereas Rosenthal has told us that Goro-vodu priests, among Ewe, explicitly state that they make their own gods, suggesting that this differentiates them from Christians, who are made by their gods, she has further suggested that Ewe understand themselves to be, in the end, sometimes "undone by their own creations" (1998: 1, 45, 223).

13. Beidelman (1993: 8) and Ashforth (2001: 219) have made similar arguments.

DOCTORS KALAMATATU

1. Ciekawy tells a similar story (2001: 174–175).

ETHNOGRAPHIC SORCERY

1. This was accentuated by the fact that my research on "traditional authority" and my research on sorcery converged on healers, with whom I spent a great deal of time during my 1999 research stint. Rasmussen (2001: xvi) has argued that most medical anthropology writings pay insufficient attention to the effects of the researcher's medical knowledge on his or her encounters with informants in the field. I played the part of the medical Good Samaritan with great ambivalence. As often as not, my medical training placed me in uncomfortable situations. Once, for example, I witnessed a man fall more than ten meters when the rotten telephone pole he was climbing (to restore phone service to the administrator's home on the occasion of the president's campaign visit to the town of Mueda in 1994) gave way beneath him. I hurried to the man's side and looked for something with which to immobilize him in order to protect his spinal column during transport to the hospital. Within a few moments, I found myself working at odds with a crowd that wished simply to pick the man up by his arms and legs and toss him in the back of a pickup truck that had stopped at the edge of the road. As I warned of the dangers

of this, others began to accuse me of trying to kill the man by delaying his transport to the hospital. Fearing, suddenly, that the crowd would turn on me, I relented and watched him be carted off. I later learned that he was released from the hospital the following day. Although he limped, he served to some as walking proof of my suspect medical sensibilities and questionable intentions.

2. Favret-Saada (1980: 11, 168–170) reported similar comments being made of her while researching witchcraft in the Bocage. See also Whitehead (2002: 32), who reported being suspected as a sorcerer for his endless inquiries on the topic.

3. Pace Jackson 1989: 8.

4. Cf. W. Davis 1988. Davis isolated and tested the substance that he suggested Haitian *bokor* used to make zombies.

5. Cf. Stoller and Olkes 1987. Stoller reported having killed someone by means of sorcery.

6. Much of what anthropologists accept as fact is bound up with their own interpretation of their informants' words, acts, and even dispositions—all the more so with a topic shrouded in innuendo, such as sorcery is in Mueda. If I speculate here about Kalamatatu's and other Muedans' understandings of ethnography and its similarity to sorcery, I do so on the basis of a wealth of interaction that contextualizes my suppositions. In any case, I seek to do what Michael Herzfeld has praised Kathleen Stewart (1996) for, namely, "juxtapos[ing] . . . 'theory-speak' with the local way of talking about events and experiences, not in order to mock either, but, to the contrary, as a way of empirically exposing the substantial intellectual grounds shared by those who study human society professionally and those who study it because that is the only way to make sense of their very conditions of life" (2001: 25).

7. Boddy has similarly compared ethnographic fieldwork and writing to spirit possession, telling us that both are "rooted in the conviction that knowledge is achieved through transcendence of the self in the other" (1989: 356–360). Eze has written: "Like the sorcerer, the anthropologist must 'escape' his world in order to encounter its objects, and fulfill the imaginary desires of his or her disciplines. Like the sorcerer, the anthropologist must also abandon his or her 'identity-constituting space' in order to make possible what is mysteriously called the 'experience of a fusing copresence of confusion.' As participant observer, and much like the sorcerer, the anthropologist must always 'face an elsewhere,' thus poised 'between inside and outside,'

in the art that seeks 'mastery of alterity.' The goal of the (re)search experience, for the sorcerer as for anthropology, is to 'uncover another world'" (2001: 273). Eze further refers to the "border-crossing" of anthropology and sorcery alike as "fantastic adventures" of "longing," "hunting," and "escaping" (273–274). See also Favret-Saada 1980: 11.

8. On this point, see Herzfeld 2001: 26.

9. Cf. Jackson 1989: 182.

10. Those who have reflected critically on the so-called crisis of representation have often assumed the resolution of this crisis to lie in collective representations deriving from "collaborative" research—from "solidarity" emerging within a dialogue between ethnographer and informant (see, e.g., S. G. Brown 2004). But even in the absence of such mutuality, I would suggest, the politics of representation need not provoke paralysis. See James, Hockey, and Dawson 1997 for a more sober assessment that recognizes the ubiquity of representation in social life and the myriad ways in which representations are challenged as a matter of course.

11. As Herzfeld has written, in praise of the work of Nicholas Thomas, "Perhaps we should stop thinking that our actions are so consequential: it is time to get matters into proportion, and this we can only do by downplaying the importance of our own roles and facing the engagement of our informants in the creation as well as the reception of our ethnographic accounts" (2001: 32).

CIRCULAR ARGUMENTS

1. Sorcerers were said to turn ordinary humans into such animals to serve their purposes.

2. Ashforth (2000: 119) has also told the story of a healer's proposition to vaccinate him.

3. Cf. Stoller and Olkes 1987: 108.

4. Green (1994: 25) has suggested that Pogoro, in Tanzania, similarly believe that the power of healing ultimately rests not in the medicinal substances used but rather in the knowledge of the healer who deploys these substances. Cf. Reynolds, who has reported that while people in Mashonaland attribute the power of healing to the healer's knowledge, healers themselves stress the importance of their "spiritual endowment" (1986: 173, 183). Cf. also Voeks, who has reported that Candomblé practitioners say that "without the leaves [medicinal substances] . . . there is no Candomblé" (1997: 160).

References

Abrahams, Ray G., ed. 1994. *Witchcraft in Contemporary Tanzania.*
Cambridge: African Studies Centre, University of Cambridge.

Adam, Yussuf. 1993. Mueda, 1917–1990: Resistência, Colonialismo,
Libertação e Desenvolvimento. *Arquivo,* no. 14:9–102.

Ardener, Edwin. 1970. Witchcraft, Economics and the Continuity
of Belief. In *Witchcraft Confessions and Accusations,* edited by
M. Douglas, 141–160. London: Tavistock.

Ashforth, Adam. 1998. Reflections on Spiritual Insecurity in a Modern African City (Soweto). *African Studies Review* 41 (3): 39–67.

———. 2000. *Madumo: A Man Bewitched.* Chicago: University of
Chicago Press.

———. 2001. On Living in a World with Witches: Everyday Epis-
temology and Spiritual Insecurity in a Modern African City
(Soweto). In *Magical Interpretations, Material Realities: Moder-
nity, Witchcraft, and the Occult in Postcolonial Africa,* edited by
H. L. Moore and T. Sanders, 206–225. London and New York:
Routledge.

Atkinson, Jane Monnig. 1989. *The Art and Politics of Wana Shaman-
ship.* Berkeley and Los Angeles: University of California Press.

Auge, Marc. 1975. *Théorie des Pouvoirs et Idéologie: Étude de Cas en
Côte d'Ivoire.* Paris: Hermann.

Bailey, F. G. 1994. *The Witch-Hunt; or, The Triumph of Morality.*
Ithaca, NY: Cornell University Press.

Basso, Keith H. 1976. "Wise Words" of the Western Apache: Metaphor and Semantic Theory. In *Meaning in Anthropology,* edited by K. H. Basso and H. A. Selby, 93–121. Albuquerque: School of American Research, University of New Mexico Press.

Bastian, Misty. 2001. Vulture Men, Campus Culturists and Teenage Witches: Modern Magics in Nigerian Popular Media. In *Magical Interpretations, Material Realities: Modernity, Witchcraft, and the Occult in Postcolonial Africa,* edited by H. L. Moore and T. Sanders, 71–96. London and New York: Routledge.

———. 2003. "Diabolical Realities": Narratives of Conspiracy, Transparency, and "Ritual Murder" in the Nigerian Popular Print and Electronic Media. In *Transparency and Conspiracy: Ethnographies of Suspicion in the New World Order,* edited by H. G. West and T. Sanders, 65–91. Durham, NC: Duke University Press.

Baum, Robert M. 1990. Reflections on a Sorcerer's Apprentice. *History of Religions* 29 (3): 297–299.

Bayart, Jean-François. 1993. *The State in Africa: The Politics of the Belly.* London and New York: Longman.

Beattie, John H. M. 1963. Sorcery in Bunyoro. In *Witchcraft and Sorcery in East Africa,* edited by J. Middleton and E. H. Winter, 27–55. New York: Praeger.

———. 1964. *Other Cultures.* London: Cohen & West.

———. 1966. Ritual and Social Change. *Man* 1:60–74.

———. 1970. On Understanding Ritual. In *Rationality,* edited by B. R. Wilson, 240–271. Oxford: Basil Blackwell.

Beidelman, Thomas O. 1963. Witchcraft in Ukaguru. In *Witchcraft and Sorcery in East Africa,* edited by J. Middleton and E. H. Winter, 57–98. London: Routledge & Kegan Paul.

———. 1989. Review of *In Sorcery's Shadow: A Memoir of Apprenticeship among the Songhay of Niger,* by P. Stoller and C. Olkes. *Ethnohistory* 36 (4): 438–440.

———. 1993. *Moral Imagination in Kaguru Modes of Thought.* Washington: Smithsonian Institution Press.

Boddy, Janice Patricia. 1989. *Wombs and Alien Spirits: Women, Men, and the Zār Cult in Northern Sudan.* Madison: University of Wisconsin Press.

Bond, George Clemente, and Diane M. Ciekawy. 2001. Contested Domains in the Dialogues of "Witchcraft." In *Witchcraft Dialogues: Anthropological and Philosophical Exchanges,* edited by G. C.

Bond and D. M. Ciekawy, 1–38. Athens: Ohio University Center for International Studies.

Bongmba, Elias K. 1998. Toward a Hermeneutic of Wimbum Tfu. *African Studies Review* 41 (3): 165–191.

———. 2001. African Witchcraft: From Ethnography to Critique. In *Witchcraft Dialogues: Anthropological and Philosophical Exchanges,* edited by G. C. Bond and D. M. Ciekawy, 39–79. Athens: Ohio University Center for International Studies.

Borges, Jorge Luis. 1970. The Circular Ruins. In *Labyrinths: Selected Short Stories and Other Writings,* 72–77. London: Penguin Books.

Bortolot, Alexander. Forthcoming. Appearance versus Reality: The Representational Turn in 20th Century Makonde Masks and Performance. PhD diss., Columbia University.

Brown, Michael F. 1986. *Tsewa's Gift: Magic and Meaning in an Amazonian Society.* Washington: Smithsonian Institution Press.

Brown, Stephen Gilbert. 2004. Beyond Theory Shock: Ethos, Knowledge, and Power in Critical Ethnography. In *Ethnography Unbound: From Theory Shock to Critical Praxis,* edited by S. G. Brown, 299–315. Albany: State University of New York Press.

Buber, Martin. 1949. *Paths in Utopia.* New York: Collier Books.

Burke, Kenneth. 1969. *A Rhetoric of Motives.* Berkeley and Los Angeles: University of California Press.

Carroll, Lewis. [1865] 1998. Alice's Adventures in Wonderland. In *Alice's Adventures in Wonderland and Through the Looking Glass.* London: Penguin Books.

———. [1871] 1998. Through the Looking-Glass. In *Alice's Adventures in Wonderland and Through the Looking-Glass.* London: Penguin Books.

Cassirer, Ernst. 1946. *Language and Myth.* New York: Dover Publications.

Castaneda, Carlos. [1968] 1990. *The Teachings of Don Juan: A Yaqui Way of Knowledge.* London: Penguin Arkana.

Chavunduka, Gordon L. 1978. *Traditional Healers and the Shona Patient.* Gwelo, Rhodesia: Mambo Press.

Ciekawy, Diane M. 1998. Witchcraft in Statecraft: Five Technologies of Power in Colonial and Postcolonial Kenya. *African Studies Review* 41 (3): 119–141.

———. 2001. Utasi as Ethical Discourse: A Critique of Power from Mijikenda in Coastal Kenya. In *Witchcraft Dialogues: Anthropolog-*

ical and Philosophical Exchanges, edited by G. C. Bond and D. M. Ciekawy, 158–189. Athens: Ohio University Center for International Studies.

Ciekawy, Diane, and Peter Geschiere. 1998. Containing Witchcraft: Conflicting Scenarios in Postcolonial Africa. *African Studies Review* 41 (3): 1–14.

Cochetti, Stefano. 1995. The Dogon Sacrifice as a Literal Metaphor. *Paragrana* 4 (2): 144–150.

Comaroff, Jean. 1985. *Body of Power, Spirit of Resistance: The Culture and History of a South African People.* Chicago: University of Chicago Press.

Cramer, Christopher, and Nicola Pontara. 1998. Rural Poverty Alleviation in Mozambique: What's Missing from the Debate. *Journal of Modern African Studies* 36 (1): 101–138.

Crawford, J. R. [1967] 1970. The Consequences of Allegation. In *Witchcraft and Sorcery,* edited by M. G. Marwick, 314–325. Harmondsworth, UK: Penguin.

Csordas, Thomas, ed. 1994a. *Embodiment and Experience: The Existential Ground of Culture and Self.* Cambridge: Cambridge University Press.

———. 1994b. *The Sacred Self: A Cultural Phenomenology of Charismatic Healing.* Berkeley and Los Angeles: University of California Press.

———. 1997. *Language, Charisma, and Creativity: The Ritual Life of a Religious Movement.* Berkeley and Los Angeles: University of California Press.

Davis, Christopher O. 2000. *Death in Abeyance: Illness and Therapy among the Tabwa of Central Africa.* Edinburgh: Edinburgh University Press for the International African Institute, London.

Davis, Wade. 1988. *Passage of Darkness: The Ethnobiology of the Haitian Zombie.* Chapel Hill: University of North Carolina Press.

de Heusch, Luc. 1985. *Sacrifice in Africa: A Structuralist Approach.* Manchester, UK: Manchester University Press.

Denzin, Norman. 1990. Review Essay: Writing the Interpretive, Postmodern Ethnography. *Journal of Contemporary Ethnography* 19 (2): 231–236.

Devisch, René. 1990. The Therapist and the Source of Healing among the Yaka of Zaire. *Culture, Medicine and Psychiatry* 14:213–236.

———. 2001. Sorcery Forces of Life and Death among the Yaka of Congo. In *Witchcraft Dialogues: Anthropological and Philosophical Exchanges,* edited by G. C. Bond and D. M. Ciekawy, 101–130. Athens: Ohio University Center for International Studies.

Dias, António Jorge, and Margot Schmidt Dias. 1970. *Os Macondes de Moçambique.* Vol. 3, *Vida Social e Ritual.* Lisbon: Centro de Estudos de Antropologia Cultural, Junta de Investigações do Ultramar.

Dillon-Malone, Clive. 1988. Mutumwa Nchimi Healers and Wizardry Beliefs in Zambia. *Social Science and Medicine* 26 (11): 1159–1172.

Durkheim, Émile. [1915] 1964. *The Elementary Forms of Religious Life.* London: Allen & Unwin.

Eliade, Mircea. 1964. *Shamanism: Archaic Techniques of Ecstasy.* New York: Bollingen Foundation.

Ellis, Stephen. 1999. *The Mask of Anarchy: The Destruction of Liberia and the Religious Dimension of an African Civil War.* New York: New York University Press.

Ellis, Stephen, and Gerrie ter Haar. 1998. Religion and Politics in Sub-Saharan Africa. *Journal of Modern African Studies* 36 (2): 175–201.

Engelke, Matthew. 2002. The Problem of Belief: Evans-Pritchard and Victor Turner on "The Inner Life." *Anthropology Today* 18 (6): 3–8.

Epstein, Scarlett. 1967. A Sociological Analysis of Witch Beliefs in a Mysore Village. In *Magic, Witchcraft, and Curing,* edited by J. Middleton, 135–154. Austin: University of Texas Press.

Evans-Pritchard, E. E. [1937] 1976. *Witchcraft, Oracles and Magic among the Azande.* Abridged ed. Oxford: Clarendon Press.

———. 1956. *Nuer Religion.* Oxford: Clarendon Press.

———. 1965. *Theories of Primitive Religion.* Oxford: Clarendon Press.

Eze, E. C. 2001. Epistemological and Ideological Issues about Witchcraft in African Studies: A Response to René Devisch, Elias Bongmba, and Richard Werbner. In *Witchcraft Dialogues: Anthropological and Philosophical Exchanges,* edited by G. C. Bond and D. M. Ciekawy, 264–282. Athens: Ohio University Center for International Studies.

Fadiman, Jeffrey. 1993. *When We Began There Were Witchmen: An Oral History from Mount Kenya.* Berkeley and Los Angeles: University of California Press.

Favret-Saada, Jeanne. 1980. *Deadly Words: Witchcraft in the Bocage.* Cambridge: Cambridge University Press.

Feld, Steven. 1987. Dialogical Editing: Interpreting How Kaluli Read *Sound and Sentiment. Cultural Anthropology* 2 (2): 190–210.

Fernandez, James. 1972. Persuasions and Performances: Of the Beast in Every Body . . . and the Metaphors of Everyman. In *Myth, Symbol, and Culture,* edited by C. Geertz, 39–60. New York: W. W. Norton & Co.

———. 1974. The Mission of Metaphor in Expressive Culture. *Current Anthropology* 15 (2): 119–145.

———. [1982] 1986. The Dark at the Bottom of the Stairs: The Inchoate in Symbolic Inquiry and Some Strategies for Coping with It. In *Persuasions and Performances: The Play of Tropes in Culture,* by J. Fernandez, 214–238. Bloomington: Indiana University Press.

———. 1991. Afterword to *African Divination Systems: Ways of Knowing,* edited by P. M. Peek, 213–221. Bloomington: Indiana University Press.

Firth, Raymond. 1966. Twins, Birds and Vegetables: Problems of Identification in Primitive Religious Thought. *Man,* n.s., 1 (1): 1–17.

Fisiy, Cyprian F. 1998. Containing Occult Practices: Witchcraft Trials in Cameroon. *African Studies Review* 41 (3): 143–163.

Fisiy, Cyprian F., and Peter Geschiere. 1991. Sorcery, Witchcraft and Accumulation. *Critique of Anthropology* 11 (3): 251–278.

———. 2001. Witchcraft, Development and Paranoia in Cameroon: Interactions between Popular, Academic and State Discourse. In *Magical Interpretations, Material Realities: Modernity, Witchcraft, and the Occult in Postcolonial Africa,* edited by H. L. Moore and T. Sanders, 226–246. London and New York: Routledge.

Forde, Daryll. 1958. Witches and Sorcerers in the Supernatural Economy of the Yako. *Journal of the Royal Anthropological Institute* 88 (2): 165–178.

Game, Ann, and Andrew Metcalfe. 1996. *Passionate Sociology.* Thousand Oaks: Sage.

Garro, Linda C., and Cheryl Mattingly. 2000. Narrative as Construct and Construction. In *Narrative and the Cultural Construc-*

tion of Illness and Healing, edited by C. Mattingly and L. C. Garro, 1–49. Berkeley and Los Angeles: University of California Press.

Geertz, Clifford. 1973. Thick Description: Toward an Interpretive Theory of Culture. In *The Interpretation of Cultures,* by C. Geertz, 3–30. New York: Basic Books.

Geschiere, Peter. 1997. *The Modernity of Witchcraft: Politics and the Occult in Postcolonial Africa.* Charlottesville, VA: University Press of Virginia.

Geschiere, Peter, and Francis Nyamnjoh. 1998. Witchcraft as an Issue in the "Politics of Belonging": Democratization and Urban Migrants' Involvement with the Home Village. *African Studies Review* 41 (3): 69–91.

Ginzburg, Carlo. [1966] 1992. *The Night Battles: Witchcraft and Agrarian Cults in the Sixteenth and Seventeenth Centuries.* Translated by J. Tedeschi and A. C. Tedeschi. Baltimore: Johns Hopkins University Press.

Goheen, Miriam. 1996. *Men Own the Fields, Women Own the Crops: Gender and Power in the Cameroon Grassfields.* Madison: University of Wisconsin Press.

Good, Byron. 1994. *Medicine, Rationality, and Experience: An Anthropological Perspective.* Cambridge: Cambridge University Press.

Goody, Esther. 1970. Legitimate and Illegitimate Aggression in a West African State. In *Witchcraft Confessions and Accusations,* edited by M. Douglas, 207–244. London: Tavistock.

Gottlieb, Alma. 1992. *Under the Kapok Tree: Identity and Difference in Beng Thought.* Bloomington: Indiana University Press.

Green, Maia. 1994. Shaving Witchcraft in Ulanga. In *Witchcraft in Contemporary Tanzania,* edited by R. G. Abrahams, 23–45. Cambridge: African Studies Centre, University of Cambridge.

Hallen, Barry. 2001. "Witches" as Superior Intellects: Challenging a Cross-cultural Superstition. In *Witchcraft Dialogues: Anthropological and Philosophical Exchanges,* edited by G. C. Bond and D. M. Ciekawy, 80–100. Athens: Ohio University Center for International Studies.

Hallen, Barry, and J. Olubi Sodipo. 1986. *Knowledge, Belief, and Witchcraft: Analytical Experiments in African Philosophy.* Stanford, CA: Stanford University Press.

Hanlon, Joseph. 1995. Report of AWEPA's Observation of the Mozambican Electoral Process. Africa European Institute/AWEPA.

Hastrup, Kirsten. 1995. *A Passage to Anthropology: Between Experience and Theory*. London and New York: Routledge.

Herzfeld, Michael. 2001. *Anthropology: Theoretical Practice in Culture and Society*. Malden, MA, and Oxford: Blackwell Publishers.

Hollis, Martin. 1970. Reason and Ritual. In *Rationality*, edited by B. R. Wilson, 221–239. Oxford: Basil Blackwell.

Horton, Robin. 1993. *Patterns of Thought in Africa and the West*. Cambridge: Cambridge University Press.

Hsu, Elisabeth. 1999. *The Transmission of Chinese Medicine*. Cambridge: Cambridge University Press.

Humphrey, Caroline, with Urgunge Onon. 1996. *Shamans and Elders: Experience, Knowledge, and Power among the Daur Mongols*. Oxford: Oxford University Press.

Israel, Paolo. 2005. Mapiko Masquerades of the Makonde: Performance and Historicity. In *East African Contours: Reviewing Creativity and Visual Culture*, edited by H. Arero and Z. Kingdon, 99–123. Critical Museology and Material Culture. London: Horniman Museum.

———. Forthcoming. Kupanga Mapiko: Danses Masquées du Peuple Makonde (Mozambique). PhD diss., École des Hautes Études en Sciences Sociales, Paris.

———. n.d. The "War of the Lions": Lion-Killings and Witch Hunts in Muidumbe (Mozambique), 2002–2003. Unpublished paper.

Jackson, Michael. 1988. Review of *In Sorcery's Shadow: A Memoir of Apprenticeship among the Songhay of Niger*, by P. Stoller and C. Olkes. *American Ethnologist* 15 (2): 390–391.

———. 1989. *Paths toward a Clearing: Radical Empiricism and Ethnographic Inquiry*. Bloomington: Indiana University Press.

———. 1996. Introduction: Phenomenology, Radical Empiricism, and Anthropological Critique. In *Things as They Are: New Directions in Phenomenological Anthropology*, edited by M. Jackson, 1–50. Bloomington and Indianapolis: Indiana University Press.

James, Allison, Jenny Hockey, and Andrew Dawson. 1997. *After Writing Culture: Epistemology and Praxis in Contemporary Anthropology*. London and New York: Routledge.

Jardine, Nick. 1980. The Possibility of Absolutism. In *Science, Belief, and Behaviour: Essays in Honour of R. B. Braithwait,* edited by D. H. Mellor, 23–42. Cambridge: Cambridge University Press.

Joralemon, Donald, and Douglas Sharon. 1993. *Sorcery and Shamanism:* Curanderos *and Clients in Northern Peru.* Salt Lake City: University of Utah Press.

Kalous, M. 1974. *Cannibals and Tongo Players in Sierra Leone.* Aukland, NZ: Wright and Carman.

Kapferer, Bruce. 1997. *The Feast of the Sorcerer: Practices of Consciousness and Power.* Chicago: University of Chicago Press.

Keane, Webb. 1997. *Signs of Recognition: Powers and Hazards of Representation in an Indonesian Society.* Berkeley and Los Angeles: University of California Press.

Kingdon, Zachary. 2002. *A Host of Devils: The History and Context of the Making of Makonde Spirit Sculpture.* London: Routledge.

Kirkmayer, Laurence J. 1992. The Body's Insistence on Meaning: Metaphor as Presentation and Representation in Illness Experience. *Medical Anthropology Quarterly* 6 (4): 323–346.

————. 1993. Healing and the Invention of Metaphor: The Effectiveness of Symbols Revisited. *Culture, Medicine and Psychiatry* 17:161–195.

Kluckhohn, Clyde. 1944. *Navaho Witchcraft.* Boston: Beacon Press.

Krige, E. J., and J. D. Krige. 1943. *The Realm of the Rain Queen.* Oxford: Oxford University Press for International Institute of African Languages and Cultures.

Laderman, Carol. 1991. *Taming the Wind of Desire: Psychology, Medicine, and Aesthetics in Malay Shamanistic Performance.* Berkeley and Los Angeles: University of California Press.

Lakoff, George, and Mark Johnson. 1980. *Metaphors We Live By.* Chicago: University of Chicago Press.

Lambek, Michael. 1993. *Knowledge and Practice in Mayotte: Local Discourses of Islam, Sorcery, and Spirit Possession.* Toronto: University of Toronto Press.

Langford, Jean M. 2002. *Fluent Bodies: Ayurvedic Remedies for Postcolonial Imbalance.* Durham, NC: Duke University Press.

Lattas, Andrew. 1993. Sorcery and Colonialism: Illness, Dreams and Death as Political Languages in West New Britain. *Man* 28 (1): 51–77.

Leach, Edmund. 1964. *Political Systems of Highland Burma*. London: Athlone Press.

Lee, Dorothy. 1959. *Freedom and Culture*. Englewood Cliffs, NJ: Prentice-Hall.

Lévi-Strauss, Claude. 1966. *The Savage Mind*. Chicago: University of Chicago Press.

Lewis, Gilbert. 1994. Magic, Religion and the Rationality of Belief. In *Companion Encyclopedia of Anthropology*, edited by T. Ingold, 563–590. London and New York: Routledge.

Lienhardt, Godfrey. 1954. Modes of Thought. In *The Institutions of Primitive Society*, edited by E. E. Evans-Pritchard, 95–107. Oxford: Blackwell.

Lindskog, Birger. 1954. *African Leopard Men*. Uppsala: Institutionen för allmän och Jämförande Etnografi.

Low, Setha M. 1994. Embodied Metaphors: Nerves as Lived Experience. In *Embodiment and Experience: The Existential Ground of Culture and Self*, edited by T. Csordas, 139–162. Cambridge: Cambridge University Press.

Luedke, Tracy J. 2005. Healing Bodies: Materiality, History, and Power among the Prophets of Central Mozambique. PhD diss., Indiana University.

Luhrmann, T. 1989. *Persuasions of the Witch's Craft: Ritual Magic in Contemporary England*. Cambridge, MA: Harvard University Press.

MacCormick, Carol P. 1983. Human Leopards and Crocodiles: Political Meanings of Categorical Anomalies. In *The Ethnography of Cannibalism*, edited by P. Brown and D. Tuzin, 51–60. Washington, DC: Society for Psychological Anthropology.

Mair, Lucy Philip. 1969. *Witchcraft*. New York: McGraw-Hill.

Marwick, Max G. 1967. The Sociology of Sorcery in a Central African Tribe. In *Magic, Witchcraft, and Curing*, edited by J. Middleton, 101–126. Austin: University of Texas Press.

Marx, Karl. [1843–1844] 1978. Contribution to the Critique of Hegel's Philosophy of Right: Introduction. In *The Marx-Engels Reader*, edited by R. C. Tucker, 53–65. 2d ed. New York: W. W. Norton & Co.

———. [1852] 1978. The Eighteenth Brumaire of Louis Bonaparte. In *The Marx-Engels Reader*, edited by R. C. Tucker, 594–617. 2d ed. New York: W. W. Norton & Co.

Meyer, Birgit. 1998. The Power of Money: Politics, Occult Forces, and Pentecostalism in Ghana. *African Studies Review* 41 (3): 15–37.

Middleton, John. 1963. Witchcraft and Sorcery in Lugbara. In *Witchcraft and Sorcery in East Africa,* edited by J. Middleton and E. H. Winter, 257–275. London: Routledge & Kegan Paul.

———. 1967. The Concept of "Bewitching" in Lugbara. In *Magic, Witchcraft, and Curing,* edited by J. Middleton, 55–67. Austin: University of Texas Press.

Middleton, John, and E. H. Winter, eds. 1963. *Witchcraft and Sorcery in East Africa.* London: Routledge & Kegan Paul.

Mombeshora, Solomon. 1994. Witches, Witchcraft and the Question of Order: A View from a Bena Village in the Southern Highlands. In *Witchcraft in Contemporary Tanzania,* edited by R. G. Abrahams, 71–86. Cambridge: African Studies Centre, University of Cambridge.

Morris, Brian. 1987. *Anthropological Studies of Religion: An Introductory Text.* Cambridge: Cambridge University Press.

Mumford, Lewis. 1922. *The Story of Utopias.* New York: Viking Press.

Myers, Gregory W., and Harry G. West. 1993. *Land Tenure Security and State Farm Divestiture in Mozambique: Case Studies in Nhamatanda, Manica, and Montepuez Districts.* Madison, WI: Land Tenure Center.

Niehaus, Isak. 2001. Witchcraft in the New South Africa: From Colonial Superstition to Post Colonial Reality? In *Magical Interpretations, Material Realities: Modernity, Witchcraft, and the Occult in Postcolonial Africa,* edited by H. L. Moore and T. Sanders, 184–205. London and New York: Routledge.

Niehaus, Isak, Eliazaar Mohlala, and Kally Shokane. 2001. *Witchcraft, Power and Politics.* London: Pluto Press.

Nietzsche, Friedrich Wilhelm. 1976. *The Portable Nietzsche.* New York: Penguin Books.

Nyamnjoh, Francis. 2001. Delusions of Development and the Enrichment of Witchcraft Discourses in Cameroon. In *Magical Interpretations, Material Realities: Modernity, Witchcraft, and the Occult in Postcolonial Africa,* edited by H. L. Moore and T. Sanders, 28–49. London and New York: Routledge.

Overing, Joanna. 1985. Today I Shall Call Him "Mummy": Multiple Worlds and Classificatory Confusions. In *Reason and Morality,* edited by J. Overing, 152–179. London: Tavistock.

Palmié, Stephan. 2002. *Wizards and Scientists: Explorations in Afro-Cuban Modernity and Tradition.* Durham, NC: Duke University Press.

Parsons, Elsie Clews. [1927] 1970. Witchcraft among the Pueblos: Indian or Spanish? In *Witchcraft and Sorcery,* edited by M. G. Marwick, 235–239. Harmondsworth, UK: Penguin.

Peek, Philip M., ed. 1991. *African Divination Systems: Ways of Knowing.* Bloomington: Indiana University Press.

Peel, J. D. Y. 1969. Understanding Alien Belief-Systems. *British Journal of Sociology* 20 (1): 69–84.

Pels, Peter. 1999. *A Politics of Presence: Contacts between Missionaries and Waluguru in Late Colonial Tanganyika.* Amsterdam, Netherlands: Harwood Adademic Publishers.

Pitt-Rivers, Julian. 1970. Spiritual Power in Central America. In *Witchcraft Confessions and Accusations,* edited by M. Douglas, 183–206. London: Tavistock.

Plotkin, Mark J. 1993. *Tales of a Shaman's Apprentice: An Ethnobotanist Searches for New Medicines in the Amazon Rain Forest.* New York: Viking.

Pratten, David. 2002. The District Clerk and the "Man-Leopard Murders": Mediating the Law and Authority in Colonial Nigeria. Paper presented at African History Seminar, School of Oriental and African Studies, London.

———. Forthcoming. *The Man-Leopard Murder Mysteries: History and Society in Colonial Nigeria.* Edinburgh: Edinburgh University Press for the International African Institute.

Rasmussen, Susan. 2001. *Healing in Community.* Westport, CT: Bergin & Garvey.

Reynolds, Pamela. 1986. The Training of Traditional Healers in Mashonaland. In *The Professionalisation of African Medicine,* edited by M. Last and G. L. Chavunduka, 165–187. Manchester: International African Institute.

Roberts, Allen F. 1986. "Like a Roaring Lion": Tabwa Terrorism in the Late Nineteenth Century. In *Banditry, Rebellion, and Social Protest in Africa,* edited by D. Crummey, 65–88. London: James Currey; Portsmouth, NH: Heinemann.

Rodman, William. 1993. Sorcery and the Silencing of Chiefs: "Words of the Wind" in Postindependence Ambae. *Journal of Anthropological Research* 49:217–235.

Rogers, Mark. n.d. "I Believe a Little Bit": Multiple Knowledges and the Politics of Medical Decisions in Ecuador. Unpublished paper.

Rosenthal, Judy. 1998. *Possession, Ecstasy, and Law in Ewe Voodoo.* Charlottesville, VA: University Press of Virginia.

Ruel, Malcolm. 1970. Were-animals and the Introverted Witch. In *Witchcraft Confessions and Accusations,* edited by M. Douglas, 333–350. London: Tavistock.

Sahlins, Marshall. 1981. *Historical Metaphors and Mythic Realities: Structure in the Early History of the Sandwich Islands Kingdom.* Ann Arbor: University of Michigan Press.

Sanders, Todd. 2001. Save Our Skins: Structural Adjustment, Morality and the Occult in Tanzania. In *Magical Interpretations, Material Realities: Modernity, Witchcraft, and the Occult in Postcolonial Africa,* edited by H. L. Moore and T. Sanders, 160–183. London and New York: Routledge.

Sanders, Todd, and Harry G. West. 2003. Power Revealed and Concealed in the New World Order. In *Transparency and Conspiracy: Ethnographies of Suspicion in the New World Order,* edited by H. G. West and T. Sanders, 1–37. Durham, NC: Duke University Press.

Sandor, Andras. 1986. Metaphor and Belief. *Journal of Anthropological Research* 42 (2): 101–122.

Sapir, Edward. [1929] 1949. The Status of Linguistics as a Science. In *Selected Writings of Edward Sapir in Language, Culture and Personality,* edited by D. G. Mandelbaum, 160–166. Berkeley and Los Angeles: University of California Press.

Sapir, J. David. 1977. The Anatomy of Metaphor. In *The Social Use of Metaphor: Essays on the Anthropology of Rhetoric,* edited by J. D. Sapir and J. C. Crocker, 3–32. Philadelphia: University of Pennsylvania Press.

Sarró, Ramon. 2000. The Throat and the Belly: Baga Notions of Mortality and Personhood. *Journal of the Anthropological Society of Oxford* 31 (2): 167–184.

Schieffelin, Edward. 1985. Performance and the Cultural Construction of Reality. *American Ethnologist* 12:707–724.

Schmoll, Pamela G. 1993. Black Stomachs, Beautiful Stones: Soul-Eating among Hausa in Niger. In *Modernity and Its Malcontents: Ritual and Power in Postcolonial Africa,* edited by J. Comaroff and J. L. Comaroff, 193–220. Chicago: University of Chicago Press.

Scott, James C. 1990. *Domination and the Arts of Resistance: Hidden Transcripts.* New Haven: Yale University Press.

Shaw, Rosalind. 1991. Splitting Truths from Darkness: Epistemological Aspects of Temne Divination. In *African Divination Systems: Ways of Knowing,* edited by P. M. Peek, 137–152. Bloomington: Indiana University Press.

———. 2001. Cannibal Transformations: Colonialism and Commodification in the Sierra Leone Hinterland. In *Magical Interpretations, Material Realities: Modernity, Witchcraft, and the Occult in Postcolonial Africa,* edited by H. L. Moore and T. Sanders, 50–70. London and New York: Routledge.

Siegel, James T. 2003. The Truth of Sorcery. *Cultural Anthropology* 18 (2): 135–155.

Simmons, William Scranton. 1980. Powerlessness, Exploitation and the Soul-Eating Witch: An Analysis of Badyaranke Witchcraft. *American Ethnologist* 7 (3): 447–465.

Soskice, Janet Martin. 1985. *Metaphor and Religious Language.* Oxford: Clarendon Press.

Stewart, Kathleen. 1996. *A Space on the Side of the Road: Cultural Poetics in an "Other" America.* Princeton: Princeton University Press.

Stoller, Paul. 1989. *Fusion of the Worlds: An Ethnography of Possession among the Songhay of Niger.* Chicago: University of Chicago Press.

———. 1995. Embodying Colonial Memories: Spirit Possession, Power, and the Hauka in West Africa. New York: Routledge.

Stoller, Paul, and Cheryl Olkes. 1987. *In Sorcery's Shadow: A Memoir of Apprenticeship among the Songhay of Niger.* Chicago: University of Chicago Press.

Synge, Richard. 1997. *Mozambique: UN Peacekeeping in Action, 1992–94.* Washington, DC: United States Institute of Peace Press.

Tambiah, Stanley Jeyaraja. 1969. Animals Are Good to Think and Good to Prohibit. *Ethnology* 8:423–459.

———. 1985. *Culture, Thought, and Social Action.* Cambridge, MA: Harvard University Press.

———. 1990. *Magic, Science, Religion, and the Scope of Social Action.* Cambridge, MA: Harvard University Press.

Tannenbaum, Nicola. 1993. Witches, Fortune, and Misfortune among the Shan in Northwestern Thailand. In *Understanding*

Witchcraft and Sorcery in Southeast Asia, edited by C. W. Watson and R. Ellen, 67–80. Honolulu: University of Hawaii Press.

Taussig, Michael. 1998. Viscerality, Faith, and Skepticism: Another Theory of Magic. In *In Near Ruins: Cultural Theory at the End of the Century,* edited by N. B. Dirks, 221–256. Minneapolis: University of Minnesota Press.

Terray, Emmanuel. 1975. Classes and Class Consciousness in the Abron Kingdom of Gyaman. In *Marxist Analyses and Social Anthropology,* edited by M. Bloch, 85–135. London: Malaby.

Thomas, Keith. 1970. The Relevance of Social Anthropology to the Historical Study of English Witchcraft. In *Witchcraft Confessions and Accusations,* edited by M. Douglas, 47–79. London: Tavistock.

Thompson, Graham. 1982. The Bewitchment and Fall of a Village Politician. *Cambridge Anthropology* 7 (2): 25–38.

Todorov, Tzvetan. 1984. *Mikhail Bakhtin: The Dialogical Principle.* Translated by W. Godzich. Minneapolis: University of Minnesota Press.

Townsley, G. 1997. Metaphors and the Unseen: The Shamanic Use of Verbal Metaphor amongst the Yaminahua of Southeastern Peru. *Cambridge Anthropology* 12 (2): 1–17.

Turner, Victor. [1957] 1996. *Schism and Continuity in an African Society: A Study of Ndembu Village Life.* Oxford: Berg.

———. 1967. Symbols in Ndembu Ritual. In *The Forest of Symbols,* by V. Turner, 19–47. Ithaca, NY: Cornell University Press.

———. 1981. Social Dramas and Stories about Them. In *On Narrative,* edited by W. J. T. Mitchell, 137–164. Chicago: University of Chicago Press.

Twitty, Anne. 1987. Review of *In Sorcery's Shadow: A Memoir of Apprenticeship among the Songhay of Niger,* by P. Stoller and C. Olkes. *Parabola: Myth, Tradition and the Search for Meaning* 12 (4): 107–110.

Urban, Greg. 1996. *Metaphysical Community: The Interplay of the Senses and the Intellect.* Austin: University of Texas Press.

Urton, Gary, ed. 1985. *Animal Myths and Metaphors in South America.* Salt Lake City: University of Utah Press.

van der Geest, Sjaak, and Susan Reynolds Whyte. 1989. The Charm of Medicines. *Medical Anthropology Quarterly* 3 (4): 345–367.

Voeks, Robert A. 1997. *Sacred Leaves of Candomblé: African Magic, Medicine, and Religion in Brazil.* Austin: University of Texas Press.

Wagner, Roy. 1975. *The Invention of Culture.* Chicago: University of Chicago Press.

———. 1986. *Symbols That Stand for Themselves.* Chicago: University of Chicago Press.

Weiner, James F. 1994. Myth and Metaphor. In *Companion Encyclopedia of Anthropology,* edited by T. Ingold, 591–612. London and New York: Routledge.

Werner, David, Carol Thuman, and Jane Maxwell. 1992. *Where There Is No Doctor: A Village Health Care Handbook.* Palo Alto, CA: Hesperian Foundation.

West, Harry G. 1997. Creative Destruction and Sorcery of Construction: Power, Hope and Suspicion in Post-war Mozambique. *Cahiers d'Études Africaines* 37 (3) (147): 675–698.

———. 2003. "Who Rules Us Now?" Identity Tokens, Sorcery, and Other Metaphors in the 1994 Mozambican Elections. In *Transparency and Conspiracy: Ethnographies of Suspicion in the New World Order,* edited by H. G. West and T. Sanders, 92–124. Durham, NC: Duke University Press.

———. 2004. Inverting the Camel's Hump: Jorge Dias, His Wife, Their Interpreter, and I. In *Significant Others: Interpersonal and Professional Commitments in Anthropology,* edited by R. Handler, 51–90. History of Anthropology, vol. 10. Madison: University of Wisconsin Press.

———. 2005a. *Kupilikula: Governance and the Invisible Realm in Mozambique.* Chicago: University of Chicago Press.

———. 2005b. Working the Borders to Beneficial Effect: The Not-So-Indigenous Knowledge of Not-So-Traditional Healers in Northern Mozambique. In *Borders and Healers: Brokering Therapeutic Resources in Southeast Africa,* edited by T. J. Luedke and H. G. West, 21–42. Bloomington: Indiana University Press.

———. Forthcoming. "Govern Yourselves!" Democracy and Carnage in Mozambique. In *Toward an Anthropology of Democracy,* edited by J. Paley. Santa Fe, NM: School of American Research.

West, Harry G., and Tracy J. Luedke. 2005. Healing Divides: Therapeutic Border Work in Southeast Africa. In *Borders and Healers: Brokering Therapeutic Resources in Southeast Africa,* edited by T. J. Luedke and H. G. West, 1–20. Bloomington: Indiana University Press.

West, Harry G., and Gregory W. Myers. 1992. Legitimidade Política à Nivel Local e Segurança de Posse da Terra em Moçambique. *Extra* (Maputo) 10:34–39.

———. 1996. A Piece of Land in a Land of Peace? State Farm Divestiture in Mozambique. *Journal of Modern African Studies* 34 (1): 27–51.

White, Landeg. 1987. *Magomero: Portrait of an African Village.* Cambridge: Cambridge University Press.

White, Luise. 2000. *Speaking with Vampires: Rumor and History in Colonial Africa.* Berkeley and Los Angeles: University of California Press.

Whitehead, Neil L. 2002. *Dark Shamans: Kanaimà and the Poetics of Violent Death.* Durham, NC: Duke University Press.

Whorf, Benjamin Lee. 1956. *Language, Thought, and Reality.* Edited by John B. Carroll. Cambridge: MIT Press.

Whyte, Susan Reynolds. 1997. *Questioning Misfortune: The Pragmatics of Uncertainty in Eastern Uganda.* Cambridge: Cambridge University Press.

Williams, Raymond. 1977. *Marxism and Literature.* Oxford: Oxford University Press.

Willis, Roy G., and K. B. S. Chisanga. 1999. *Some Spirits Heal, Others Only Dance: A Journey into Human Selfhood in an African Village.* Oxford and New York: Berg.

Wilson, Monica. [1951] 1970. Witch-Beliefs and Social Structure. In *Witchcraft and Sorcery,* edited by M. G. Marwick, 276–285. Harmondsworth, UK: Penguin.

Winch, Peter. 1970. Understanding a Primitive Society. In *Rationality,* edited by B. R. Wilson, 78–111. Oxford: Basil Blackwell.

Index